I0424220

The New Gods

The New Gods:

Psyche and Symbol in Popular Art

Harold Schechter

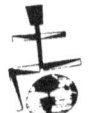

Bowling Green University Popular Press
Bowling Green, Ohio 43403

Acknowledgements

I wish to thank the Research Foundation of the City University of New York for the grants which made it possible for me to spend several summers working full-time on this project and to travel to the Center for the Study of Popular Culture, Bowling Green State University. The director of the Center, Ray Browne, has been a constant source of encouragement. I owe him a great debt of gratitude.

I owe a similar debt to many people in the English department of Queens College, and particularly to four friends who have been very supportive of my work: Morris Dickstein, Don McQuade, Bill Kelly, and Charles Molesworth. I would also like to thank Doris Albrecht of the C.G. Jung Foundation for her generous assistance, Robert Crumb for his continuous kindness, and Stan Willard for helping me prepare the illustrations for the book.

Parts of this book have appeared in earlier versions in various publications, including *The Psychocultural Review* and *San Jose Studies*. I am grateful to the editors of these journals for allowing me to reprint this material. I am also grateful to the following people and publishers for permission to use their work:

Houghton Mifflin Company, Boston, for excerpts from James Dickey's *Deliverance.*

Highlights for Children, Columbus, Ohio, for *Goofus and Gallant*, copyright © 1973.

D.C. Comics for panels from "In the Beginning," *SHAZAM!*, copyright © 1972.

Marvel Comics for panel art from "Midnight Brings Dark Death", *Master of Kung Fu*, copyright © 1974.

R.Crumb for panels from "Whiteman," "Squirrely the Squirrel," and "Pete the Plumber."

Princeton University Press for the woodcut from *Rosarium Philosophorum, Secunda Pars Alchemiae de Lapide Philosophico* (Frankfurt, 1550). Collection of Dr. C.A. Meier.

Daniela Gioseffi for poems from her book *Eggs in the Lake*, Brockport, N.Y.: BOA Editions.

Eggs Ackley among the Vulture Demonesses

Copyright © 1980 by Bowling Green University Popular Press

The New Gods is a trademark of D.C. Comics, Inc. used under license.

For Jonna

CONTENTS

Unpalatable though it may be to modern taste, the truth is that we cannot live without the early gods... If cast out in the forms of Man's profoundest apprehensions of them—if Christ and Buddha and Mithra, if Ashtaroth and Pan are disowned—they nevertheless come back. However meanly and unrecognizably, they come back to the human heart whose inevictable tenants they are. And "there all smothered up in shade" they sit, radiating that strange compelling power which is Man's unconscious tribute to the Unknowable.

Alan McGlashan, "Daily Paper Pantheon"

Introduction

In such an age, *our* age, it is not surprising that the books which move the young are essentially religious books, as, indeed, pop art is always religious.
                                        Leslie Fiedler, "Cross the Border—Close the Gap"

When the old gods died, there arose—the New Gods!
                                        Jack Kirby, *The New Gods* (No. 1)

1

IN A BOOK called *Myths to Live By,* Joseph Campbell considers the origin of such Biblical "anamolies" as the creation of Eve, the Fall, and Noah's flood—episodes in a history which never happened but which has compelled belief for centuries. "Who invents these impossible tales?" Campbell wonders, speaking of religious mythologies in general. "Where do their images come from? And why—though obviously absurd—are they everywhere so reverently believed?"[1]

The present study is an attempt to answer the same set of questions about the "impossible tales" and images of popular art—the space odysseys and extraterrestrial civilizations, the caped crusaders and men of steel and monsters from the ocean floor. The very fact that these same questions can be asked of both religious myth and popular entertainment seems significant to me, suggesting that, in terms of their ultimate source, appeal and even their meaning, the two are closely connected. While such a link between the sacred and profane—the Good Book and the comic book—might strike many people as silly or even offensive, it is immediately apparent to anyone who has ever, say, attended one of the annual meetings of comic collectors that take place in New York City every Fourth of July weekend.

These gatherings have the character of true congregations— assemblages of devotees, who will jostle each other for a glimpse of a *Superman no. 1* or stand breathlessly before an early *All Star Comics* exhibited under glass. Though his use of the phrase is meant to be playful, Stan Lee, the editor-in-chief of Marvel

1

Comics, hits on something essential when he addresses his readers as "True Believers"—as he does, for instance, in the introduction to his book *Origins of Marvel Comics:* "So read on, O True Believer. May this small but salient slice of living history now serve to nourish thine awestruck, hungry eyes."[2] Despite the condescending cuteness of his language, Lee's remark accurately conveys the scriptural significance his publications possess for many readers.

Similarly, one need only visit a convention of *Star Trek* fans—"Trekkies," as they call themselves—to be forcibly reminded that the word "fan" is short for "fanatic" (which in turn derives from the Latin *fanaticus,* meaning "of a temple" or "inspired by a god"). Even the people connected with the show—which stopped production in 1968 but has been rerun continuously on local TV stations ever since—have been bemused by its profound and persistent appeal.

"I really don't understand it," remarked William Shatner, the star of the series, after speaking at a Trekkie convention. "I was asked to appear in an auditorium of some 8,000 to 10,000 people, there just because of *Star Trek*. They were crazed. I don't know why the fanaticism has attached itself to the show. . . . Why this is happening defies rational explanation."[3] Gene Roddenberry, the program's creator, also returned from one of these conventions astonished at "the near fanatical cult that continues to follow the series." "It is scary," he told an interviewer, "to be surrounded by a thousand people asking questions as if the events in the series actually happened."[4]

According to Robert Jewett and John Shelton Lawrence, authors of a book called *The American Monomyth,* the zeal of the *Star Trek* fans—who believe in the truth of the scripts the way theologians believe in the Scriptures—has all the hallmarks of religious devotion, and accordingly, they characterize the phenomenon as "Trekkie Religion."[5] They defend this description by pointing to such proof as the "outbursts of ecstasy" the show produces in its followers; the "personal redemptive experiences" which many of them report (*"Star Trek* has changed my life. . . ," etc.); and the elaborate "fanzine" (i.e., fan magazine) literature which has developed around the program and which—in "spinning out *Star Trek* episodes . . . to see what happened beyond the revelational scope of the original television series"—

bears striking similarities to "apocryphal literature in the biblical tradition. This kind of writing answers essentially theological questions, amplifying and illustrating a faith." The authors conclude that, though "a popular belief has...arisen that the religious impulse is dead," phenomena "like *Star Trek*'s popularity suggests an alternative hypothesis. Religion may have merely changed its theater and neglected to place its name on the marquee. The move from the cathedral to the tube, screen, or stereo offers the faithful many of the values sought in traditional religion."[6]

This "move from the cathedral to the tube, screen, or stereo," this transformation of divinity into diversion, has been noted by other scholars as well. In his book *Myths, Dreams, and Mysteries,* for example, Mircea Eliade asks, "What has become of myths in the modern world?"—and his answer is in part that they are to be found in our amusements, that they "survive among our contemporaries in more or less degraded forms."

Noting that, through his participation in myth and ritual, primitive man is able to escape from the passage of time, to enter a deathless, eternal world, Eliade argues that the same "magico-religious" function is served in modern society by our entertainments, our "distractions"—by those things we do to "kill time." "It seems that a myth itself," he says, "never disappears...it only changes its aspect and disguises its operations."[7]

Alan McGlashan, a British psychiatrist, comes to the same conclusion in a brief but provocative piece which appeared in *The Lancet* in 1953. Entitled "Daily Paper Pantheon," the article points out some striking parallels between "the early gods" and the characters in certain comic strips then appearing in the London *Daily Mirror.*[8]

At least one major pop artist seems to have intuited the truth that McGlashan sets down in this essay—that the fantasy figures of popular culture are the latest incarnations of the primordial gods. In 1971, Jack Kirby, the creator of such modern mythic heroes as Captain America and the Fantastic Four, brought out a remarkable "trilogy" of comic books titles, consisting of *The New Gods, Forever People,* and *Mr. Miracle*—an ambitious attempt to create, within the confines of the comic book format, an entire mythological system. The cover of the first issue of *The New Gods* proclaimed, "When the old gods died, there arose—the New Gods!" By so naming his creations, Kirby had, for the first time in the comics themselves, made the submerged spiritual significance of the popular culture "superhero" explicit.

2

McGlashan's observation—that the ultimate source of all these figures, the comic strip characters as well as the gods, is "Man's unconscious"—brings us back to Joseph Campbell's original question and the starting point of this study. "Who invents these impossible tales?" Campbell asks. "Where do their images come from?" And his answer, like McGlashan's, is that they are emanations from the deep mind of man: "For they are not historical. That much is clear. They speak, therefore, not of outside events but of themes of the imagination. And since they exhibit features that are actually universal, they must in some way represent features of our general racial imagination, permanent features of the human spirit—or, as we say today, of the psyche."[9]

In using such phrases as "the deepest level of the human psyche" and "our general racial imagination," both McGlashan and Campbell point to the theory which provides us, I believe, with the greatest insight into the significance and appeal of the popular arts: Carl Jung's theory of the archetypes of the collective unconscious.

The concept of the archetype has been misunderstood by a great many people, partly because Jung's own formulations often seem to contradict one another. Throughout his writings, he describes archetypes in various ways—as "primordial images," "inherited thought-patterns," "imprints" or "regular physical occurrences," "self-portraits" of the instincts, etc. This ambiguity, I believe, is the result of Jung's own career-long effort to find a precise linguistic equivalent for an intuited concept that is essentially inarticulable. One thing which he does make very clear, however, is that the archetypes are *not* "racial memories," inherited recollections of man's ancestral past. They are, rather, inborn *tendencies*—which all humans share—to produce certain symbols. In his book *C.G. Jung and the Scientific Attitude*, Edward G. Cohen provides a concise definition of Jung's major theory: "Briefly stated," he writes, "the hypothesis of the collective unconscious is that *there are universal symbols and myths which are a function of the nature of the psyche itself;* accordingly, they are produced by different people in different times and places...."[10]

As a result of his observations of parallel "myth-motifs" surfacing in the fantasies of individuals widely separated in space and time, Jung advanced the thesis that "just as the human body shows a common anatomy over and above all racial differences, so, too, the human psyche possesses a common substratum transcending all differences in culture and consciousness."[11] He theorized that, beneath the "personal unconscious"—that repository of repressions identified by Freud—there exists a deeper level of the mind which is inborn and *trans*personal. This is the collective unconscious: a "timeless and universal psyche" containing "the whole spiritual heritage of mankind's evolution, born anew in the brain structure of every individual."[12]

According to Jung, the collective unconscious is composed of archetypes—innate structures which predispose us to perceive and respond to the world in specifically human ways. These fundamental factors, which "make up the groundwork" of the human personality, are closely related to, and are perhaps best understood by comparison with, animal instinct. In the first volume of his tetratology *The Masks of God,* for instance, Joseph Campbell describes the behavior of newly born chicks which "dart for cover when a hawk flies overhead, but not when the bird is a gull or duck, heron or pigeon." This instinct he calls "the image of the inherited enemy," which is "always sleeping in the nervous system, and along with it the well-proven reaction."[13]

This reaction, explains Campbell, illustrates the fact "that in the central nervous system of all animals there exist innate structures that are somehow counterparts of the proper environment of the species."[14] Jung makes a similar point in his essay "On the Nature of the Psyche": "There are in fact no amorphous instincts," he writes, "as every instinct bears in itself the pattern of its situation.... The instinct of the leaf-cutting ant fulfills the images of ant, tree, leaf, cutting, transport, and the little ant garden of fungi.... Such an image is an *a priori* type. It is inborn in the ant prior to any activity, for there can be no activity at all unless an instinct of corresponding pattern initiates and makes it possible."[15]

What is true of the chick and the ant, Jung argues, is likewise true of man: he also "has in him these *a priori* instinct types which provide the occasion and the pattern for his activities, in so far as he functions instinctively. As a biological being, he has no choice but to act in a specifically human way and fulfill his pattern of behavior."[16] The human mind, that is to say, is not a *tabula rasa:* we too are born with inner correspondences to our environment. We come into this life, Jung argues, "prepared for a quite definite world where there is water, light, air, salt, carbohydrates, etc. The form of the world into which [man] is born is already inborn in him....Likewise parents, wife, children, birth, and death are inborn in him as...psychic aptitudes."[17]

These "psychic aptitudes," these innate neurological structures "that constitute the elementary foundations of all human experience and reaction,"[18] Jung calls the archetypes as such (*an sich*). They are, as he states repeatedly, forms without content. But like all unconscious factors, they tend to manifest themselves symbolically, "clothed" in the images of conscious experience and projected into dreams, fantasies, and imaginative products of every kind. Thus the *archetypal images* or *symbols* can be described, according to Jung, as "the pictorial forms of the instincts" or "the self-portrait[s] of the instinct[s]."[19]

A somewhat fanciful example may help to make this concept more clear. Let us look again at the case of the freshly hatched chick, cited by Campbell. Built into its central nervous system is an innate structural element which prepares the newborn bird for a world containing hawks and makes possible the appropriate instinctive response to its enemy. This element is the "archetype" of the hawk in the chick's nervous system.

The living hawk which sets off the self-protective response, however, is not in itself an archetypal image. To understand what the archetypal image is, we must imagine a chick capable of creating religion and art. The chick's deity (or devil) would very likely be some all-powerful Hawk God (or Demon)—represented perhaps as an awesome black shadow with wide-flung wings, fierce and all-seeing. And this representation would be the archetypal image: i.e., the projection, in pictorial form, of the archetypal/instinctual complex residing deep in the "soul" of the chick, the symbolic expression of how the chick *experiences* hawks. (Thus, according to Jung, the archetypal image "represents the *meaning* of the instinct.")[20] Since all chicks would come into this world possessed of a "hawk archetype," the same symbol (with slight variations) might be produced by any chick in the world at any time in history. And all chicks would respond deeply to the sight of it. Any actual hawk would then be, in a sense, a living manifestation or incarnation of the mythic Hawk God.

Let us now translate our imaginary model back into human terms. Consider, for example, the *mother archetype.* The archetypal image—*Magna Mater,* the Great Mother Goddess—is the projection into myth of the deeply unconscious archetypal/instinctual complex which all of us are born with, our innate readiness to respond to a mother (not to a particular mother but to the experience of mother, to the maternal). Anyone's actual mother is not, clearly, an archetypal image, but the *bearer* of this image—i.e., an "embodiment" of it. The child's perception of his mother, that is to say—and even (though to a lesser degree) the adult's—is inevitably colored by his projection of this powerful image onto the living woman.

In Jung's view, then, *all* mythological images are projections of the collective unconscious. As the symbolic expression of the most fundamental level of the human mind, such images are possessed of enormous power or "numinosity," exerting a "compelling effect" on every beholder. We know we are in the presence of primordial images, Jung tells us, by "an instinctive feeling of significance"—"something deep in us is stirred."[21]

Moreover, since these symbols are, in Edward G. Cohen's words, "a function of the nature of the psyche itself," they will be produced by people in all ages and cultures. Of course, the archtetype *as such* only determines the form, the underlying structure, of the symbol, and not its specific content, which varies from culture to culture; so that, while all hero figures, for example, are fundmentally alike, an ancient Greek hero will appear as a bearded demi-god draped in a lion skin and bearing a club, whereas a late twentieth-century American hero might be a "bionic man," his superior powers bestowed on him, not by the lords of Olympus, but by their contemporary counterpart, the great god Technology.

But whatever their particular shape, these images will arise from the depths of the psyche "wherever creative phantasy is freely manifested."[22] As Erich Neumann, the distinguished Jungian analyst puts it, "the archetype is a mythological motif and...as an 'eternally present' content of the collective—i.e., universal human—unconscious, it can appear equally well in the theology of Egypt or the Hellenistic mysteries of Mithras, in the Christian symbolism of the Middle Ages or the visions of a modern psychotic."[23] Or, for that matter, in a comic book, TV show or film.

That certain works of popular art derive their "curiously compulsive power" from archetypes is not a new theory. Jung himself suggests as much in his essay "Psychology and Literature," where he argues that, in terms of mythological content, Rider Haggard's *She* is as rich and resonant a work as *Moby-Dick* or *Faust*. In another essay, "On the Psychology of the Trickster-Figure," he makes note of McGlashan's piece, observing that "the figures in comic strips have remarkable archetypal analogies."[24] More recently, Northrop Frye, Leslie Fiedler and the science fiction writer Ursula K. Le Guin have all pointed out that popular art is essentially mythic. In *Anatomy of Criticism*, Frye defines popular literature as "literature which affords an unobstructed view of archetypes."[25] Fiedler, in a piece called "To Be in Dreams Awake," maintains that "the medium is not the message in popular art—far from it. The medium is in some sense irrelevant to the message popular art, since popular art works in a very striking way by...evoking primordial images."[26] And in an article entitled "Myth and Archetype in Science Fiction," Le Guin examines some of the stock characters of pop culture—"the blonde heroes of sword and sorcery, with their unusual weapons...mad scientists...detectives who found out who done it...brave starship captains...evil aliens; good aliens; and every pointed breasted brainless young woman who was ever rescued from monsters..."—and concludes that "their roots are the roots of myth, are in our unconscious—that vast dim region of the psyche and perhaps beyond the psyche, which Jung called 'collective' because it is similar in all of us, just as our bodies are basically similar."[27]

Le Guin, however, stops short of defining these popular

fantasy figures as truly mythological, referring to them instead as "submyths," since "they have the vitality of the collective unconscious but nothing else, no ethical, aesthetic, or intellectual value." In a sense, of course, Le Guin is merely making the same point here that Jewett and Lawrence, Eliade, and McGlashan all make: that in our rationalistic, materialistic, secular society, the old mythic figures—whom we may deny but can never do utterly without—are forced to sneak in through the back door. If "the early gods" have disappeared from our religions, they can still be seen nightly on network TV or found everyday in the funnies.

Le Guin (strangely enough, for one of our most popular writers of science fiction and fantasy) does not seem to have much use for television, comic strips or most other popular forms, regarding them as "grotty." While I consider this judgment excessively harsh, it does raise an important issue—that of the aesthetic quality of popular art. It seems undeniable to me that popular art in general is indeed aesthetically inferior to what we call "high" culture. To maintain that a *Spider-Man* comic, for example, is an art object with the depth and complexity of *Moby-Dick* (or even *The Deerslayer*) is clearly untenable.[28] Nevertheless, the comparative artistic crudeness of the former does not automatically relegate it to the realm of trash. For as Le Guin herself perceives, the roots of both the comic and the classic are ultimately the same; aesthetically, the two may have nothing in common, be miles apart—but there *is* a level on which they come together and may be legitimately compared, and that is the level of myth and dream. And it is precisely that level which Jungian theory allows us to explore. Far from being "mindless escapism" or "worthless junk," popular art is a projection of the collective unconscious—an expression of the deepest, myth-producing level of the human psyche.

Chapter One

Individuation and Popular Art

1

> The mysterious way leads inwards.
> Novalis, *Fragment*

ONE OF JUNG'S most important discoveries was that the archetypes are not merely images but *dynamisms* which direct our lives in deeply unconscious but purposive ways. The archetypes, that is to say, are experienced not only as symbols emerging in dream, fantasy, myth and art, but also as autonomous and transpersonal powers motivating human behavior. In his classic study *The Great Mother,* Erich Neumann discusses the "compelling character" of the archetype—how "it determines human behavior unconsciously but in accordance with laws and independently of the experience of the individual"[1]—and cites as an example "the archetype of the 'way.' " "As far as we know," writes Neumann,

this archetype first appeared among the prehistoric men of the ice age. In a ritual that was still in large part unconscious, the way led these early men into mountain caves, in whose hidden and almost inaccessible recesses they established 'temples' adorned with representations of animals on the killing of which their existence depended.

The magical and sacral significance of these paintings and of the caves in which they are found is today unquestioned. But it is also evident that the "hard and dangerous way," by which alone these caves could often be reached, formed a part of the ritual reality of the mountain temples that we now see in them.

At a later cultural stage, when consciousness was more highly developed, this archetype of the way became a conscious ritual. In the temple precinct, for example...the worshiper is compelled to follow a ritual way from the periphery to the shrine. Christ's Calvary is another, more highly developed form of this archetype... Moreover, ths symbol of the archetypal way has taken a universal place in the consciousness and orientation of modern man. We take for granted such expressions as "inner ways of development"; and the companion symbols of "orientation" and "disorientation"...belong to the same context. All these linguistic formulations are based on the archetype of the way, whose pattern determines the originally unconscious behavior of man moving toward a sacred goal.[2]

Neumann—and Jung too—insists on the religious quality of

the archetypes, their "numinosity," their power to "seize and possess the whole personality."[3] To traditional man, this power, through the mechanism of projection, was experienced as emanating from a divine force outside himself—from God. For modern man, however, God is dead and the great religious symbols of the West have lost their *mana*. As a result, we have become, in the words of Jungian analyst Edward F. Edinger, severed from "the suprapersonal forces which are the source of our being and our meaning."[4] According to Jungian psychology, then, the primary—indeed critical—goal of modern man must be to rediscover the gods within, to integrate his alienated ego with the transpersonal powers of the deep unconscious.

The means of achieving this integration in known in Jungian terms as "the way of individuation," a process of psychological development symbolized by the mythic hero's quest or "night sea journey," whose primary stages are indentified by Joseph Campbell as "separation-initiation-return."[5] Departing from the workaday world, the hero travels to the "threshold of adventure. There he encounters a shadow presence that guards the passage. The hero may defeat or conciliate this power and go alive into the kingdom of the dark . . . or be slain by the opponent and descend in death."[6] Within this underworld, the hero passes through a series of initiatory ordeals ("the Road of Trials"), achieves the boon he has been seeking ("the Treasure Hard to Attain"), and returns, transfigured, to the daylight. This age-old and ubiquitous story— called by Campbell "the monomyth"—is, Jungians tell us, a metaphor for the individuation process: an "initiation into inner reality"[7] involving the ego's heroic descent into the depths of the psyche and its encounter with the dangerous but potentially revivifying contents of the collective unconscious. In its earliest stages, individuation has the same goal as psychoanalysis: namely, the raising of repressed personal complexes to consciousness. The second and far more difficult phase consists of a confrontation with those fundamental psychic factors (i.e., the archetypes) which form the general human basis of our individual personalities. John Halverson summarizes the concept as making the union of ego and archetype,[8] in which individuation "gives rise to an integrated consciousness in which the body-mind antithesis is no longer allowed to individual personalities—particularly the *shadow* (the "lower primitive, instinctual" half of the psyche) and the *contrasexual* ("the 'anima' for men, and for male-dominated civilization in general").[8] By effecting the union of ego and archetype, individuation "gives rise to an integrated consciousness in which the body-mind antithesis is no longer allowed to function.... Those instinctual processes most opposed to consciousness are gradually assimilated by it."[9] "In this way," writes Jung, "there arises a consciousness which is no longer imprisoned in the petty, oversensitive, personal world of the ego, but participates freely in the wider world of objective interests."[10] This "widened consciousness," which Jung calls the *Self* ("a term that is meant to include the totality of the psyche in so far as this manifests itself in an individual"), is the ultimate treasure awaiting any individual courageous enough to endure the terrors of the voyage into "No Man's Land"—the "country beyond the ego."[11]

Individuation was, Jung felt, a fundamental impulse within the human psyche—an innate urge satisfied in the past through religious myth and ritual, which provided the believer with a symbolic system for achieving union with "the numinous 'other'."[12] For "modern man in search of a soul," psychoanalysis—or, more accurately, analytical psychology, which is the name Jung gave to his method to distinguish it from Freud's—offers the best hope of self-realization. The psychiatrist, as Joseph Campbell puts it, "is the modern master of the mythological realm, the knower of all the secret ways and words of potency," guiding the quester—the seeker after self-knowledge—through the torturous windings of the dark, psychic underworld.[13] It is also possible, according to Jungian theorists, for certain exceptional people to achieve individuation "naturally," i.e., "without using special methods or needing guidance."[14] Such individuals include those artists who "accomplish the individuation process...in their artistic work, the work reflecting the process."[15]

Jung's ideas on artistic creativity are the logical outgrowth of his theory of psychic structure. As we have seen, he conceived of the mind as a system divided into separate (though interdependent) "strata," and throughout his writings he distinguishes between different kinds of imagery (whether appearing in dreams, fantasies or literary productions), according to the level of the psyche from which the images ultimately derive. In his essay "On the Nature of Dreams," for example, Jung—following the custom of certain primitive tribes—categorizes dreams as either "little" or "big." The former, which might also be called personalistic, "are the nightly fragments of fantasy coming from the subjective and personal sphere, and their meaning is limited to the affairs of everyday life." "Big" ("meaningful," mythological) dreams, on the other hand, arise from a "deeper level" of the psyche—the collective unconscious—and "contain symbolical images which we also come across in the mental history of mankind," i.e., the archetypes of the individuation process.[16] The distinction Jung draws here between "little" and "big" dreams corresponds very closely to his classification of literary works as either "psychological" or "visionary." By psychological fiction Jung means those books which "deal with materials drawn from the realm of human consciousness—for instance, with the lessons of life, with emotional shocks, the experience of passion and the crises of human destiny in general—all of which go to make up the conscious life of man and his feeling life in particular."

The visionary novel, on the other hand, usually consists of "an exciting narrative that is apparently quite devoid of psychological exposition." It portrays events which "astonish" us, "evokes a superhuman world of contrasting light and darkness," reminds us of "nothing in everyday life, but rather of dreams, night-time fears, and the dark recesses of the mind that we sometimes sense with misgiving." "Mythological themes clothed in modern dress also frequently appear." Like those dreams which he designates "big," visionary literature, according to Jung, has its ultimate source in the archetypal psyche: "that which appears in [visionary art] is the collective unconscious." The creation of such art, that is to say, consists of *"an unconscious animation of the archetype, and... a development and shaping of this image till the work is completed."*

Perhaps the most significant feature of Jung's literary theory, however, is his hypothesis that archetypes appear in works of art in response to specific psychological needs: "What is of particular importance for the study of literature in these manifestations of the collective unconscious," he maintains, "is that they are compensatory to the conscious attitude. This is to say that they can bring a one-sided, abnormal, or dangerous state of consciousness into equilibrium in an apparently purposive way."[17]

What Jung claims in this passage, then, is that the presence of "primordial imagery" in a work of art signifies an attempt by the collective unconscious to correct some psychological deficiency—to effect the realization of the self. I will have more to say about the compensatory function of mythological art in a later chapter. For now, the part of Jung's theory I wish to stress is his notion that visionary art strives to promote, through symbolic means, the integration of the personality—or, to put it another way, that individuation is the underlying, psychological theme of all visionary (archetypal) art.

That myths themselves symbolize the way of individuation is the thesis set forth by Joseph Campbell in *Hero With a Thousand Faces*. Though Campbell does not use the phrase "individuation process," he defines the psychological meaning of the "monomyth" in specifically Jungian terms. "The first work of the hero," he writes, "is to retreat from the world scene of secondary effects to those causal zones of the psyche where the difficulties really reside, and there to clarify the difficulties, evaluate them in his own case (i.e., give battle to the nursery demons of his local culture) and break through to the undistorted, direct experience and assimilation of what C.G. Jung has called 'the archetypal images.' "[18]

Similarly, Edward F. Edinger maintains that "when the Christian myth is examined carefully in the light of analytical psychology, the conclusion is inescapable that the underlying meaning of Christianity is the quest for individuation."[19] Fairy tales, too, according to Jungian thought, represent the struggle for self-realization. In her book, *An Introduction to the Interpretation of Fairy Tales,* for example, the analytical psychologist Marie-Louise Von Franz flatly states that "all fairy tales endeavor to describe one and the same psychic fact.... This unknown fact is what Jung calls the Self, which is the psychic totality of the individual...."[20]

That archetypal fiction also portrays the individuation process can be seen clearly in the case of *Moby-Dick*—one of the examples of visionary art cited by Jung in his essay "Psychology and Literature." At least four important Jungian analyses of

Melville's work have been written—James Kirsch's "The Enigma of *Moby-Dick*," Martin Pops' *The Melville Archetype*, John Halverson's "The Shadow in *Moby-Dick*," and, most recently, Edward F. Edinger's *Melville's Moby-Dick: A Jungian Commentary*—and all concur that Melville's novel "describes the archetypes in the collective unconscious and possible ways of relating to them."[21] *Moby-Dick*, according to this view, grew out of its author's intense yearning for a spiritual experience which traditional religious symbols could no longer provide—a yearning which propelled him on an inward quest, culminating in his discovery of the "gods as psychic factors."[22]

What Jung makes very clear in "Psychology and Literature," however, is that it is not only literary masterpieces which can be classified as "visionary." As I pointed out in the introduction, along with *Moby-Dick* and *Faust*, Jung includes the fiction of H. Rider Haggard among his examples of works in the "visionary mode." He also mentions "that most popular article of literary mass-production, the detective story, first exploited by Conan Doyle."[23] While it may seem scandalous to apply as exalted a term as "visionary" to potboilers and "literary mass-productions," the fact remains that Jung's two categories of artistic creation can be applied as easily to popular culture as to high.

In the expanded version of "Daily Paper Pantheon" which appears in his book *Savage and Beautiful Country,* for example, Alan McGlashan makes a distinction between "realistic" comic strips like *Blondie* and *Peanuts*, which "satirically reflect the modern scene," and those comics which are characterized "by the presence of an element of the miraculous or magical"—comics which, deriving their "images from a...mysterious source," exert "a curiously compulsive power, overriding rational repudiation, on the minds of multitudes."[24] Since this "mysterious source," as McGlashan goes on to argue, is the mythological level of the human psyche, we should expect to find—in accordance with Jung's theory—that such comic strips symbolically portray the process of individuation. Of course, it is (in McGlashan's words) "painful to contemplate" the idea that a meaning communicated in the past through myths, folk tales and visionary art should come to us today through the "cheap and paltry" images of popular culture.

But, as we have previously suggested, in a secular age such as ours, spiritual values must disguise themselves in order to survive. "It is a mark of our neglect," writes McGlashan, "that these values are forced to put on so mean a mask in order to reenter human consciousness.... The comic strip is, in fact, a ludicrous but valid symptom of our disease."[25] When the established forms of religion cease to function in any meaningful way for a culture, the gods are driven underground and take up their residence in despised and subterranean regions: "low" culture and the "lowly" unconscious.

The closest modern-day equivalents of the ritual Neumann describes—the initiatory passage through the mysterious way— are activities like the fraternity hazing and the trip through the amusement park Fun House; and gods once clothed in glory now dress up in the tawdry costumes of comic book "superheroes." Nevertheless, to the degree that popular art embodies archetypal images (as I believe that much of it does), its essential theme is the same as that of our highest works of art: the theme of man's perennial struggle to achieve an integrated Self—to establish a harmonious relationship with those immanent, super-personal powers which sustain and give meaning to human existence.

2

Billy stood awed before the ancient one. The seated figure spoke, and, although the comics were a printed medium, I could hear his voice, cracking and aged...yet carrying the authority of the mighty and the righteous. (For how many years was that printed visage my personal vision of God?)

Dick Lupoff, "The Big Red Cheese"

A work which affords excellent insight into the symbolic meaning of popular art is "In the Beginning," the "retelling" of the Captain Marvel "legend" which appears in the comic book SHAZAM! (no. 1).[26] While the draftmanship in certain contemporary comics is surprisingly sophisticated, "In the Beginning" is drawn (by artist C.C. Beck) in a simple (though energetic), "primitive" style which makes it a kind of comic book equivalent of the fairy tales collected in the original edition of the

Grimm Brothers' *Kinder- und Hausmärchen*. Friedrich Schiller once wrote that "Deeper meaning resides in the fairy tales told to me in my childhood than in the truth that is taught by life,"[27] and while I'm not prepared to make an assertion as sweeping as Schiller's, it is my contention that—as is the case with fairy tales—the meaning of many comic books is far deeper than one might expect, given the comparative naivete of the form.

A little historical background is necessary before we turn our attention to the story at hand. The creation of writer Bill Parker and artist C.C. Beck, Captain Marvel made his first appearance in *Whiz Comics*, no. 2 (1940), and soon became the most popular of the costumed superheroes. "The World's Mightiest Mortal" (as he was called), Captain Marvel was, in reality, newsboy Billy Batson, who could transform himself into the Herculean hero simply by uttering the magic word SHAZAM (the meaning of which will be explained below). Despite—or rather because of—his popularity, Captain Marvel disappeared from the comic book scene in the mid-1950s, the victim, not of his archfoe, the nefarious Dr. Sivana ("The World's Wickedest Scientist"), but of his prototype and prime competitor on the comic book marketplace, Superman. Piqued by the success of the Captain Marvel series (which was issued by Fawcett), the publisher of *Superman*, National Comics, sued Fawcett for copyright infringement. The case dragged on in court for years (with renowned lawyer Louis Nizer representing Superman's side) until Fawcett, in an out-of-court settlement, agreed to discontinue the Captain Marvel adventures.

Ironically, the character was revived twenty years later in *SHAZAM!* magazine, published by none other than National Comics.[28] "In the Beginning"—the lead story in the first issue of *SHAZAM!*—is a "frame tale" set within Billy Batson's elaborate explanation for his twenty-year disappearance (having to do, not with the mundane facts of the case, but with Captain Marvel's supposed abduction and long imprisonment by Dr. Sivana). The story starts out with a character named Mr. Binder, who, while strolling down a city street, encounters his old acquaintance, Billy. To Binder's astonishment, Billy—though "missing for twenty years"—has not aged a day. As Binder wanders off, convinced he is going crazy, Billy commences to narrate his remarkable history.

Appropriately, the first line of the story is much like the traditional opening—"Once upon a time"—of the fairy tale. "It all started a long time ago," Billy begins. Like the typical fairy tale hero, Billy is an orphan. And, though the setting of the story is a modern metropolis—presumably New York—it bears little resemblance to an actual city. Rather, with its blank, shadowy features, it is the urban equivalent of the dark, haunted forest of such fairy tales as "Snow White," "Little Red Riding Hood," and "Hansel and Gretel": a magical dreamscape symbolizing, according to Bruno Bettelheim, "the need to find oneself."[29]

In the visual vocabulary of the comic books, Billy's story—though we are meant to accept it as actual history—seems to take the shape of a fantasy or dream. Its beginning is framed within a "balloon" whose cumulous cloud-shaped outline is meant to suggest that the image is issuing from inside Billy's mind: supposedly a memory but just as easily a dream. The opening image (fig. 1) is certainly dreamlike. One cold, rainy night, Billy stands on a streetcorner (unprotected, without hat, coat or umbrella), "hawking" newspapers. The city seems utterly deserted: even the severity of the weather cannot account for the absolute emptiness, the spooky stillness of the streets. To whom is he peddling his papers? The scene has the threatening atmosphere common to the bad dreams of the city dweller, who, in his nightmares, will find himself lost and defenseless in a sinister section of town. In literature, this motif finds powerful expression in the work of the American romantics—Brown, Hawthorne, Melville—whose young heroes often undergo dark nights of the soul as they wander through the labyrinthine streets of ominous cities.

As he stands on the corner, Billy is suddenly surprised by a voice calling out to him "Pssst! Lad—come here!" Turning, he sees a man silhouetted against the bright entrance of a nearby subway tunnel. This "mysterious figure" is dressed from top to toe in black; though his shape is more sharply defined, he is as dark and one-dimensional as the long shadow he casts before him onto the rain-slicked sidewalk. With his coat collar pulled up around his neck and his high-peaked hat drawn low over his face, his features are completely obscure. "It's late," he says to Billy. "Why aren't you home in bed?" "I have no home, sir," the boy politely replies. Billy's industry and courtesy—like his orphaned state—are typical traits of the fairy tale hero.

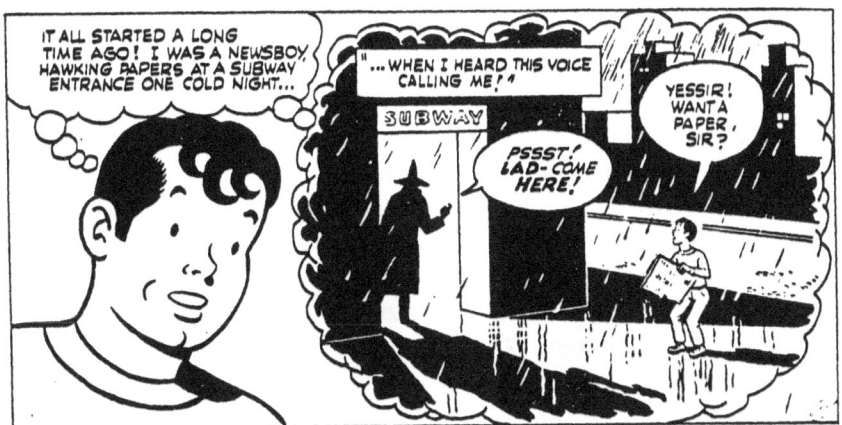

Reprinted with permission from D.C. Comics for panels from "In the Beginning," *SHAZAM!*, copyright © 1972.

In "The Water of Life," for example, which David Adams Leeming describes as the "clearest" portrayal of the individuation process among the Grimm Brothers' stories, the young hero (though in this case not an orphan) is helped on his quest for the magic elixir by a dwarf whose question—"Where are you going?"—the hero answers with humility and respect. This young prince, like "all heroes of the quest," represents, in Leeming's words, "our potential journey of discovery into the unconscious."[30] Billy, too, is such a quest hero, and his homeless and orphaned condition is a further sign of his psychic significance, symbolizing the rootlessness and isolation of an ego which has yet to attain the wholeness of the Self.

The beginning of Billy's quest takes the archetypal form of the journey into the underworld, traditionally represented by the passage into a cave (" a metaphor for the mysteries of the human heart . . . as old as literature itself," according to Leslie Fiedler),[31] but symbolized here—as is appropriate in an updated, urbanized fairy tale—by the descent into the subway. At this stage, the dark stranger lurking in the subway entrance plays the mythological part of the threshold guardian who must be dealt with before the hero can continue on his way.

The roads of mythic heroes from Oedipus to Bilbo Baggins have run by the dwelling places of dangerous creatures, who require that the hero solve a riddle, answer a question, piece together a puzzle—in short, pass some sort of test—before he can proceed. "In a myth of the Melanesian island of Malekula in the New Hebrides," writes Joseph Campbell, "which describes the dangers of the way to the Land of Death, it is told that when the soul has been carried on a wind across the waters of death and is approaching the entrance of the underworld, it perceives a female guardian sitting before the entrance, drawing a labyrinth design across the path, of which she erases half as the soul approaches. The voyager must restore the design perfectly if he is to pass through it to the Land of the Dead."[32] Billy "conciliates" the guardian by responding satisfactorily to the stranger's question, and, as a result, is permitted to cross the threshold and enter the region of the unknown.

Accompanied by the mysterious figure—who serves now as the *psychopomp*, the mythological guide, "the one who shows the way"[33]—Billy is "led...into a murky, abandoned tunnel" (fig. 2). As the hero and his guide make their way down the decaying, cobweb-covered staircase, the black, one-dimensional stranger seems less like a separate being than the boy's misshapen shadow thrown against the tunnel wall. The moment they reach the bottom of the stairs, "a strange subway car, with headlights gleaming like a dragon's eyes," suddenly roars into the station and stops (fig. 3). "Have no fear," the stranger reassures Billy. "A mystic power will guide us safely!"

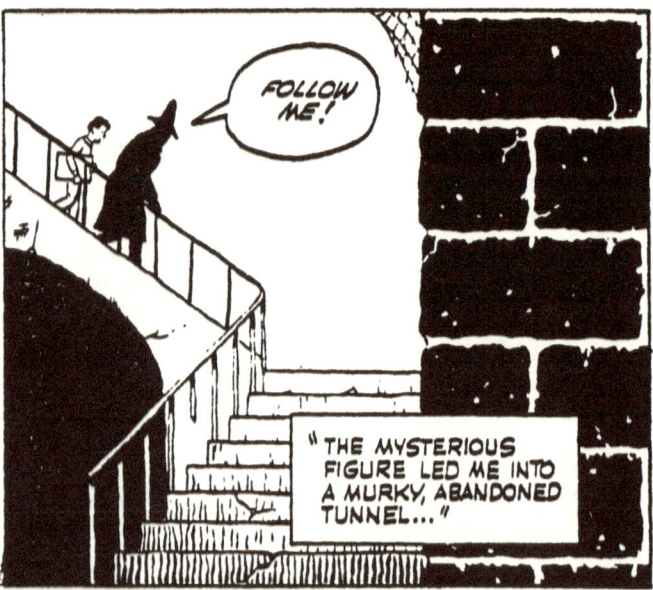

Reprinted with permission from D.C. Comics for panels from "In the Beginning," *SHAZAM!*, copyright ᶜ 1972.

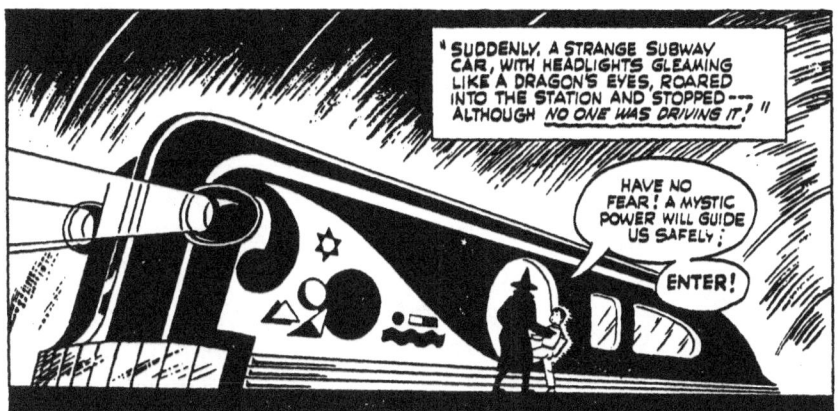

Reprinted with permission from D.C. Comics for panels from "In the Beginning," *SHAZAM!*, copyright ᶜ 1972.

Billy's entrance into this supernatural subway train —with its beams like the eyes of a dragon, grillwork like a mouth bristling with teeth, and sleek, serpentine "body" covered with mysterious symbols—is analogous to the common mythological motif in which the hero is devoured by a monster: an image, as Joseph Campbell, Northrop Frye and others have pointed out, of the descent into hell. "The descent is...often portrayed as a mimic, temporary or actual death of the hero," writes Frye; "or he may be swallowed by the dragon, so that his descent is into the monster's belly. In medieval treatments of the Christian story some of these themes reappear. Between his death on the cross and his resurrection Jesus descends into hell, often portrayed, especially in fresco, as the body of a huge dragon or shark, which he enters by the mouth, like his prototype Jonah."[34]

That Billy's journey through the subway is indeed a voyage to hell becomes clear the moment he steps from the train. Having arrived at "the end of the line," he is conducted by his "mysterious companion" through the mouth of a cavern and into an "ancient underground hall, carved out of solid rock and lit by flaring torches" (fig. 4). What marks this place as a comic book vision of Hades is the group of seven tall statues, each with a blazing fire at its feet, which lines one wall of the passageway: allegorical figures representing "The Seven Deadly Enemies of Man" Pride, Envy, Greed, Hatred, Selfishness, Laziness, Injustice. Garishly colored in shades of blue, green, yellow, and red, and grimacing comically, like the totems of a tribe of Three Stooges' fans, these

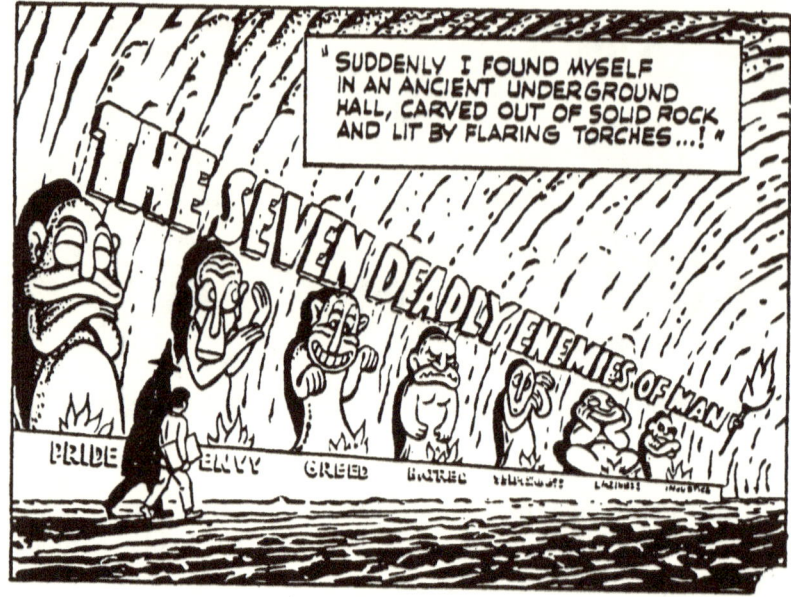

Reprinted with permission from D.C. Comics for panels from "In the Beginning," *SHAZAM!*, copyright © 1972.

statues are, of course, the Seven Deadly Sins.[35] To be sure, they appear in a burlesque and bowdlerized form: gluttony and lust have been replaced by selfishness and injustice, and the monitory phrase "the deadly enemies of man" has been substituted for the specifically theological "sins."

If this is an updated *Inferno*, it is one whose language and visual imagery are drawn, not from Dante and Gustave Doré but from the pages of the official Boy Scout Handbook. Throughout the story there is a good-humored juxtaposition of the sublime and the ridiculous, a combination of Biblical solemnity and schoolyard playfulness epitomized by the title: "In the Beginning: A Retelling of the Greatest Legend in Comics." It is likely, of course, that the original pre-teen readers of the comic took its mock-reverential tone seriously and responded to the tale with childlike awe. But even for adult readers, I believe, Billy's experience—repeating as it does the archetype adventure story of the great religious and mythological heroes of the world—resonates with a special, if subconscious, meaning, for all that it has been trivialized through its translation into a popular culture idiom.

As Neumann points out, the "hard and dangerous way" winding through the darkness of the underworld leads, ultimately, to a "sacred goal." Billy's underground journey also brings him to a sacred spot, for when he reaches the end of the tunnel he finds himself at the foot of a "great throne," seated upon which is a "majestic figure" who identifies himself as "Shazam, an ancient Egyptian wizard," but who, as Dick Lupoff and other young readers have long recognized, is clearly God.[36] An iconological analysis of the panel in which Billy confronts the kingly old man leaves little room for doubt about the wizard's identity (fig. 5). From the vantage point of his raised seat Shazam can gaze down upon the earth floating off, to his right; while on the left, leaning against the side of the throne, is a giant, leather-bound volume: the fabled Big Book of the child's imagination, in which God keeps score of one's good deeds and bad.[37] "For thousands of years I have fought evil, Billy Batson," says the white-haired patriarch (who, incidentally, looks not the least bit like an Egyptian—let alone an *ancient* Egyptian—though that nationality does endow him with a suitably Semitic aura). "H-how did you know my name?" asks the boy; to which Shazam replies, "Because I know *everything!*"

At a glance, it might seem illogical for Billy to meet God in a subterranean chamber since such divine encounters traditionally occur in much loftier locations, which the hero reaches by climbing a celestial staircase or scaling a mountain, not by going

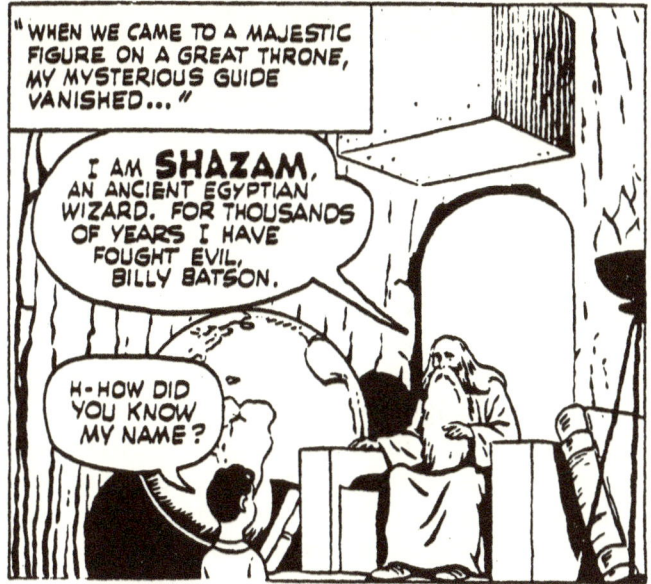

Reprinted with permission from D.C. Comics for panels from "In the Beginning," *SHAZAM!*, copyright © 1972.

down into a cave. Northrop Frye, however, in an essay entitled "New Directions from Old," sheds a good deal of light on this seeming inconsistency. Writing about the cosmologies found in medieval and Renaissance poetry, Frye explains that "In Dante, in Spenser, in Milton, the foreground of symbols and images seems to be portrayed against a background of roughly four levels of existence"—a background to which Frye applies the term "topocosm." The uppermost of these levels "is the place of the presence of God, the empyreal heaven, which operates in this world as the order of grace and providence," while the bottommost "is the level of sin, death and corruption." "Throughout this period," writes Frye, "it was traditional to symbolize the top level by the starry spheres, the spiritual by the physical heaven." Frye goes on to argue, however, that

after the rise of Copernican astronomy and Newtonian physics, the starry sky becomes a less natural and more perfunctory and literary metaphor for the spiritual world. The stars look increasingly less like vehicles of angelic intelligences, and come to suggest rather a mechanical and mindless revolution....A deity at home in such a world would seem stupid or malignant....Hence the variety of stupid sky-gods in Romantic poetry: Blake's Urizen, Shelley's Jupiter, Byron's Arimanes, Hardy's Immanent Will, perhaps the God of the Prologue in *Faust*.

With the rise of Romanticism, then, we find the creation of a new "topocosm"—"almost the reverse of the traditional one"—in which the highest level "is the bleak and frightening world of outer space," while the lowest, "corresponding to the traditional hell or world of death, is the mysterious reservoir of power and life out of which both nature and humanity proceed." As an example of this second "topocosm," Frye refers to *Prometheus Unbound*: "In the sky is Jupiter, the projection of human superstition with its tendency to deify a mechanical and sub-human order...and at the bottom of the whole action is the oracular cave of Demogorgon, who calls himself Eternity, and from whom the power proceeds that rejuvenates Earth, liberates Prometheus, and annihilates Jupiter."[38]

The universe of "In the Beginning" conforms in a very striking way to the reverse, Romantic "topocosm" described by Frye, not only because the underworld is the abode of an omnipotent and life-giving power—Shazam—but also because, as it turns out, the place of evil, the realm of the "mechanical and sub-human" is the sky, where the "World's Wickedest Scientist," Dr. Sivana, commits his crimes from the orbiting refuge of a spacecraft equipped with the technological fruits of his evil genius: "Vortex transporter paralyzer beams" and other "devilish devices."

Before Billy can do battle with Sivana, however, he must win the boon bestowed on all mythological heroes. This—the achievement of the "Treasure Hard to Attain"—is, in Campbell's words, the "culminating episode" of the quest.[39] Though the reward traditionally assumes a wide variety of forms in myth, ritual, folklore and legend, it is always representative of the same spiritual acquisition: "Intrinsically it is an expansion of consciousness and therewith of being (illumination, transfiguration, freedom)."[40] The "culminating episode" of "In the Beginning," actually combines several familiar forms of the "Treasure" motif. First, there is that "triumph" which Campbell calls "Atonement with the Father." "I have chosen you to be my successor," the old wizard informs Billy. "M-me sir?" replies the astonished boy. "Yes," says Shazam. "You are pure of heart!" With that, the ancient Egyptian commands the young hero to "Speak my name!" "Shazam!" cries Billy, whereupon a cosmic explosion occurs—"A thunderclap from the ends of the universe...an eye-searing bolt of magic lightning"—and the orphaned newsboy is instantly transformed into, reborn as, "The World's Mightiest Mortal": Captain Marvel, whom Jules Feiffer nicely describes as a "friendly fullback of a fellow with apple cheeks and dimples,"[41] dressed (in typical superhero fashion) in skin-tight red leotards, handsomely complemented with golden belt, boots, and wristbands and a white satin cape draped over one shoulder.

As "campy" as this episode is—as far removed in tone as it is from the stories of Phaëton, Dionysos, Christ and Job which Campbell cites as examples—it nevertheless reproduces exactly the same archetypal image of father-son "at-one-ment" portrayed in the great religious myths of the world. The otherworldly, omniscient patriarch selects a boy who is "pure at heart" and bestows on him the magical boon of the father's name: Shazam. By speaking it—a symbolic act of identification with the father— the hero is transfigured, changed from a child into a more-than-human being whose supramundane nature is symbolized by the bolt of "magic lightning" emblazoned on his chest, and whose mission is to succeed Shazam as the scourge of "all evil on earth." What happens to Billy matches in every respect Campbell's description of the final stage of the hero's initiatory quest, "his recognition by the father-creator (father atonement)": "The mystagogue (father or father-substitute) is to entrust the symbols of office only to a son who has been effectively purged of all inappropriate infantile cathexis—for whom the just, impersonal exercise of powers will not be rendered impossible by unconscious (or perhaps even conscious and rationalized) motives of self-aggrandizement, personal preference, or resentment. Ideally, the invested one has been divested of his mere humanity and is representative of an impersonal cosmic force. He is the twice-born: he has become himself the father."[42]

Billy's assumption of Shazam's place is represented in the comic by the old man's bodily disappearance the moment the boy's metaphorsis into Captain Marvel takes place. "So it is written that I must go," says the wizard, seating himself again on the throne. "And in the same unbelievable instant," as Billy puts it, an immense block of stone hanging "by a thread" directly over the old man falls with a crash, apparently obliterating him. Captain Marvel is grieved ("P-poor old guy...."), but in fact his mentor has not been destroyed. Shazam's divine, immortal nature—which up until this point has merely been implied by his great age and omniscience—is now explicitly revealed, for as the smoke from the crashing block clears, Captain Marvel sees before him the "ethereal form" of the wizard.

The climactic moment of the hero's initiation is at hand. As "The World's Mightiest Mortal" stands at attention, his spiritual father points a finger at him and proclaims, "I dub you Captain Marvel! Through my name you are given the powers of these six mighty heroes!" Like the novices in primitive puberty ceremonies—which have been described at great length by Campbell, A.W. Howitt, Arnold Van Gennep, Mircea Eliade, Bruno Bettelheim and others—Billy receives a new name to symbolize his rebirth.[43] And—as is also true of archaic puberty rituals, which always lead up to the novice's initiation into the sacred mysteries of his tribe, to the revelation of closely guarded religious secrets—Billy's experience culminates in his acquisition of esoteric knowledge: the meaning of the magical word Shazam stands revealed to him, carved on a great stone tablet which either hangs on or (it is difficult to tell) is actually a part of the chamber wall (fig. 6).

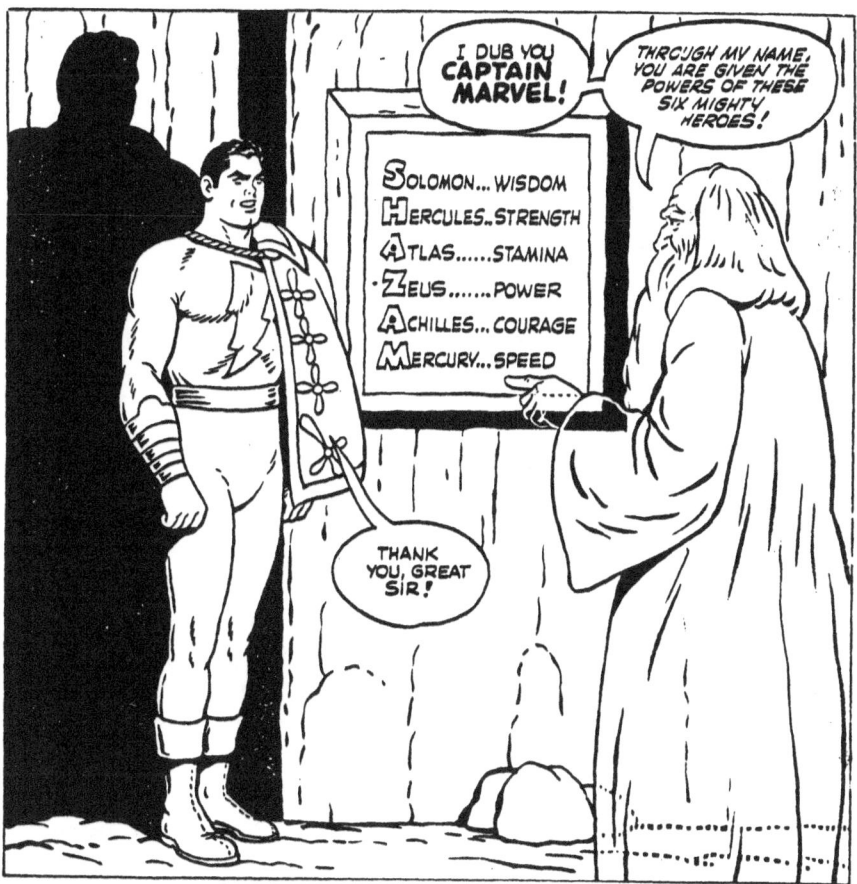

Reprinted with permission from D.C. Comics for panels from "In the Beginning," *SHAZAM!*, copyright © 1972

This acronym "Shazam," which takes the names of great heroes and gods and turns them into a child's nonsense word, is a very interesting construction. Like the story it appears in, it evokes a host of mythological associations while at the same time making them into something playful—something, however, which still communicates part of the power of its mythic components. Though the mixture of Biblical and Classical references in the acronym is confusing, to say the least (particularly when we recall that Shazam serves as the name of an ancient Egyptian), the word is nevertheless another indication of its owner's mythico-religious character. (It is interesting, incidentally, that the iconography of this panel subtly reinforces the story's religious meaning. To the right, standing in the foreground—a position which makes him look monumental, even larger than the mighty Captain Marvel—is the immaterial figure of Shazam. His raised left hand seems to be both pointing to the hero and presenting him with the tablet, which apparently has been carved out of the rock wall of the chamber. This tablet is, in effect, divided in two, with a row of six words running down the left side and a parallel row on the right. If the earlier panel, in which Billy confronts the old wizard for the first time, represents a child's view of God sitting on his heavenly throne, this scene suggests nothing so much as a kindergarten version of the Lord presenting Moses with the Tables of the Law.) For Captain Marvel, learning the secret of Shazam's name is equivalent to gaining access to the source of divine power and wisdom. This is the second boon the hero is given, and, having received it, he is sent back into society to do his "father's" work.

That a piece of popular culture as simple and unsophisticated as "In the Beginning" should resonate with religious symbolism is a fact which many people will always find hard to accept; others, however, have begun to discern the deeper meanings which even the most lighthearted entertainments can sometimes conceal. In an article on the latest screen version of the Superman saga, for example, *Newsweek* magazine's film reviewer, Jack Kroll, discusses the "inescapable tilt" of that movie "toward myth and messianism." "People can croak 'Entertainment! Entertainment!' until they're blue in the face," he writes. "The fact remains that films like 'Close Encounters of the Third Kind,' 'Superman,' and even 'Star Wars' have become jerry-built substitutes for the great myths and rituals that cultures used to shape before mass secular society took over." After describing some of the more overtly religious moments in the movie (such as the scene in which Superman resurrects Lois Lane, who has died in an earthquake, and another in which the spirit of his father informs him that "Earthlings can be a great people, they only lack the light; for this reason I've sent them you, my only son"), Kroll concludes:

Superman as the son of God, as the Saviour, as the Resurrection and the Life? Isn't that appallingly vulgar, a grisly reflection of the junk culture that has just about buried real culture almost out of sight? I don't believe it is. Why shouldn't these great revelatory myths come back into the collective consciousness in the most effective ways that our civilization...has set up?[44]

Like the legend of Superman—upon which (as the famous lawsuit established) it was modelled—the story of Captain Marvel's origin has a symbolic dimension which lifts it out of the category of "mere entertainment." As a piece of children's fiction which conveys surprisingly complex, subconscious meanings, "In the Beginning" has affinities not only with fairy tales but also with the symbolic classics of American literature, which, as Leslie Fiedler pointed out long ago, "are notoriously at home in the children's section of the library, their level of sentimentality precisely that of a pre-adolescent."[45] Given what Fiedler describes as "the regressiveness, in a technical sense, of American life, its implacable nostalgia for the infantile, at once wrong-headed and admirable,"[46] it is perhaps inevitable (as Kroll suggests in his remarks about *Superman*) that, in our culture, myth should appear in such a childlike form.

Be that as it may, "In the Beginning" is a story rich in significance, not only because it embodies mythic archetypes but also because it shows how modern man—spiritually rootless, isolated in his egocentricity—can reestablish a connection with those large, sustaining forces which, in times past, were made accessible through the rituals of organized religion. What Billy's night journey reveals is that the gods, though degraded, have not disappeared; to find them, however, we must look inward instead of upward: into the depths of the unconscious. This comic book, in short, portrays the process of individuation or psychic initiation: the inner quest which, by leading to the integration of ego and archetype, produces that enlargement of the personality, that state of psychic wholeness, which Jung calls the Self.

Billy's transformation from a child into a titan—a being bursting with energy and at one with the gods—represents the psychological rebirth, the expansion of consciousness, that results from the ego's assimilation of the archetypes. This new state of psychic integrity is manifested in the massive and indestructible physique the hero gains, an image equivalent to the "diamond body" of Chinese alchemy which, as Jung shows, is symbolic of the integrated Self.[47] The sense of "absolute, binding, and indissoluble communion" with transcendent powers which individuation produces is signified in the story by Billy's progression from an orphan into Son-of-Shazam. According to Jung, as a result of individuation, "the original state of oneness with the God-image [i.e., the Self] is restored. It brings about an integration, a bridging of the split in the personality caused by the instincts striving apart in different and mutually contradictory directions."[48]

That the wizard himself represents an ideal image of wholeness, of psychic integration, is made clear by the acronym which serves as his name and which stands for the integration of various spiritual and instinctual powers. Even Captain Marvel's costume is significant in this respect. Given his football player's physique, the skin-tight red leotards and satin cape seem, in their effiminacy, laughably incongruous. Though the ambiguous sexuality of the costumed superhero has been attacked as a subconscious incitement to homosexual behavior,[49] my own feeling is that it is the equivalent of the ritual transvestism which is a common feature of primitive initiation rites (and which can also be found in literary works dealing with the theme of initiation; *The Adventures of Huckleberry Finn,* for instance, has a hero who, for one chapter at any rate, turns into a girl).[50] It is, in other words, a symbol of the psychological androgyny, the integration of the masculine and feminine principles, which is another characteristic of self-realization (and about which I will have more to say later on).

"In the Beginning," then, is a story which portrays with great clarity the "way of individuation." Even the start of Billy's adventure—his unexpected encounter with the black, mysterious being who has emerged from the depths of the subway tunnel—corresponds precisely to Jung's description of the individuation process. This sinister stranger, who stands at the threshold of the unconscious, is an example of the figure Jung calls the *shadow*—the embodiment of the dark, "unacceptable" side of the psyche, which must be faced and acknowledged before further insight can be achieved. "The meeting with oneself," Jung writes, "is at first the meeting with one's own shadow"[51]—and as we shall see in the following chapter, this archetypal encounter is one of the most pervasive themes in popular art.

Chapter Two

The Realization of the Shadow

1

Every man casts a shadow; not his body only, but his imperfectly mingled spirit. This is his grief. Let him turn which way he will, it falls opposite to the sun; short at noon, long at eve.

Henry David Thoreau
A Week on the Concord and Merrimack Rivers

SYMBOLIC STORIES of every kind—myths, fairy tales, and "visionary" works, both popular and high—teach us that the meeting with the shadow marks the start of self-discovery. "The shadow" is the term Jung applied to an archetypal image known by many different names: the stranger, the other, the alien, the alter-ego, the doppelgänger. Whatever this image is called, however, its psychological significance is always the same. The shadow is the symbol of the personality's dark, socially unacceptable side—of that part of ourselves we feel to be so shameful or threatening that we have trouble acknowledging it as our own. The Jungian analyst Frieda Fordham defines the shadow as "the inferior being in ourselves, the one who wants to do all the things that we do not allow ourselves to do, who is everything that we are not, the Mr. Hyde to our Dr. Jekyll."[1]

The shadow, in short, is a personification of those repressed fantasies, impulses and desires which constitute what Jung calls the *personal unconscious*: the "evil self" which, as the name of Dr. Jekyll's alter-ego indicates, we keep hidden from the world and even from ourselves. Meeting the shadow, then, whether such a

31

meeting occurs to a character in a story or to a patient in analysis, always signals the possibility, at least, of self-realization; for it means that the individual has come face to face for the first time with a side of himself that he has never directly confronted—has never been ready or willing to confront—before.

In each of our lives, this archetype manifests itself in a number of ways. First, as Fordham suggests, the shadow makes itself felt in those moments when we seem to be possessed by an alien personality. Depth psychology teaches us that the more strenuously we repress our impulses and emotions the more energy they build up in the unconscious and the more urgently they press for some sort of release. If denied too fiercely, they are bound to burst out in a destructive or disconcerting way: in an explosion of anger, say, which leaves us shaken and astonished by its intensity, or in an embarrassing "Freudian slip" which makes us feel as though some mischievous entity, who is bent on humiliating us and over whom we have absolutely no control, has spoken through our mouths. Because of its autonomous quality, Jung conceives of the shadow as a separate "splinter personality" demanding recognition from the ego: "The shadow is a part of the personality and therefore wants to live with it in some form," he writes. "It cannot be argued out of existence or rationalized into harmlessness."[2]

When an individual is incapable of recognizing his shadow, however—unable to live with the dismaying truth about himself—he will generally protect himself against such painful awareness by *projecting* his shadow traits onto the people around him; he will maintain the illusion of his moral perfection by seeing his own despised, unconscious qualities someplace in the world outside, where he can safely and self-righteously condemn them. When we find ourselves intensely and irrationally loathing a person we scarcely know, we can be sure that what we are really perceiving in this individual is some negative trait that we cannot bear to face up to in ourselves. Hawthorne's Young Goodman Brown is a perfect example of a man who flees in horror from his single glimpse of his soul's shadow side, and thereafter defends himself against the recognition of his own guilt-ridden impulses by attributing them to everyone but himself.

Besides manifesting itself in possession and projection, the shadow can also be seen, in our day-to-day lives, in dreams, where it appears in personified form as "a dark figure of the same sex as the dreamer"[3]—a figure that, despite its strange, sinister, or even repulsive qualities, nevertheless often seems dimly, disconcertingly familiar. In dreams (as well as in myths and fairy tales) this figure assumes certain typical guises, which embody the shadow's psychological characteristics.

For example, as the "evil half" of the personality, the shadow is frequently symbolized by a diabolical double or evil twin; while, as the psyche's "foreign side," it may take the form of a foreigner, alien, or mysterious stranger. (At times, these two forms of the archetype may overlap, so that it is possible, in dreams as well as in literature, for an individual to encounter a sinister stranger who turns out to be a long-lost sibling. In fiction, Hawthorne's story "Alice Doane's Appeal" is an excellent example.) As the "primitive, instinctual, sensual" part of the human soul,[4] the shadow often appears as a wild, brutish or animalistic being. And sometimes—since the shadow comprises "inferior traits of character" which society regards with contempt—it is represented as a "servant or 'lower' man."[5] In the dreams (and imaginative products) of white people, the shadow, as the "dark side" of the personality, often takes the form of a non-white character; in the case of Americans, Jung discovered, it is commonly symbolized by "a Negro or an Indian."[6]

All the forms of the shadow archetype which are found in dreams are common to classic literature as well. Moreover, wherever this archetype appears—in a play by Shakespeare, a novel by Melville, or a short story by Dostoyevsky, Conrad, Hawthorne or James—it always conveys the same symbolic meaning. This is not to say that "The Secret Sharer," "The Jolly Corner," and *Benito Cereno,* for example, have interchangeable themes. But insofar as all three deal with what Jung calls "the realization of the shadow"—with the idea of a man discovering for the first time a dark, previously unsuspected side of his own personality and of the human soul in general—they all portray the dangers of denying the shadow and the benefits of acknowledging its existence and accepting it as a part of one's life.

Clearly the reactions of different fictional characters to the meeting with their shadows vary widely. But in every case, those characters who cannot or will not come to terms with the "horror" they uncover end up spiritually destroyed (like Melville's Spanish captain or Hawthorne's Young Goodman Brown); while those who are able to live with and even befriend the shadow are revitalized as a result. "Not ignoring what is good," says Ishmael in the very first chapter of *Moby-Dick*, "I am quick to perceive a horror, and could still be social with it...since it is but well to be on friendly terms with all the inmates of the place one lodges in."[7] Soon after, he meets and embraces the cannibal Queequeg, and immediately the melancholy young narrator—whose "hypos" have grown so severe that he has begun "pausing before coffin warehouses and bringing up the rear"of funeral processions— experiences a kind of rebirth, feels himself "redeemed" and reinvigorated by the "soothing savage"[8] who had appeared so appalling at first sight. For the fact is that the shadow—however ugly or terrifying it might seem when we first confront it—also contains those primitive, instinctual energies from which civilized man cuts himself off at great peril, at the cost of his health, wholeness and spontaneity. The "shadowless life," as Calvin S. Hall and Vernon J. Nordby observe, inevitably becomes "shallow and spiritless"—devoid of vitality.[9] Self-realization, therefore, can only be achieved by those who, like Ishmael, can be "social" with the shadow; who can say, as Prospero says of the brutish Caliban at the end of *The Tempest,* "This thing of darkness I / Acknowledge mine."[10]

While the meeting with the shadow is a recurrent motif in "high" literature, the number of popular works in which it appears—movies, television shows, comic books, and so forth—is virtually limitless. Northrop Frye's definition of popular literature as "literature which affords an unobstructed view of archetypes" applies to every form of "mass art," which, in general, presents archetypal characters and situations with very little aesthetic elaboration or adornment. One of the reasons that "pulp" novels, for example, can be turned out so quickly and in such quantity—as compared to serious fiction—is that the hack writer pays so little attention to technique; instead, as Henry Nash Smith points out in his discussion of the "dime novelists" of the late nineteenth century, the author "abandons his own personality and identifies himself with the reveries of his readers." "Fiction produced in these circumstances," says Smith, "virtually takes on the character of automatic writing"; it becomes "an objectified mass dream, like the moving pictures, the soap operas, or the comic books that are the present-day equivalents" of the dime novels.[11] As Leslie Fiedler says, "the medium is not the message in popular art," which tends to portray "primordial images" in a plain, unselfconscious style. Moreover, these images are not only embodied very baldly in popular art, they are also repeated obsessively, the same basic archetypes appearing again and again like recurrent dream symbols through which highly charged unconscious contents press urgently for recognition.

Thus, while it would be relatively easy to compile a list of classic stories dealing with the theme of the shadow in its various manifestations (alter-ego, doppelgänger, etc.), a comparable list of popular works—of horror movies featuring a scientific mastermind with a monstrous alter-ego; of melodramas about the conflict between a pair of rival brothers, one good, one evil; of fantasies in which the hero confronts a fiendish facsimile of himself, created through science or sorcery; of Westerns in which a white-clad cowboy does battle with a gunslinger who dresses all in black—would be impossible to produce.

But if "the medium is not the message in popular art," then what is? It seems to me that the underlying psychological meaning that popular art tries to convey so insistently to consciousness is the same one found in such "visionary" classics as "The Jolly Corner," "The Secret Sharer" and *Moby-Dick:* namely, the importance of coming to know and learning to live with the unexplored parts of the personality, beginning with the shadow. At times, popular art conveys this message quite explicitly. For example, in an episode of the television series "Star Trek" entitled "The Enemy Within," a bizarre accident (involving a malfunctioning "transporter beam") splits Captain Kirk, the commander of the starship *Enterprise,* into two, antipathetic people, one timorous and weak, the other violent and brutish. Naturally enough, neither of these individuals alone is capable of managing the vessel, since the former is ineffectual and the latter is mindlessly animalistic. Disaster, however, is averted when a means of recombining the separated halves of the captain is found.

Kirk (one of whose functions in the program is to mediate between the hyperrational Mr. Spock and the excitable Dr.

McCoy: to serve, that is to say, as an ideal embodiment of wholeness, of the integration of logic and emotion, intellect and instinct) regains his confidence, self-possession and power to act. He becomes once more the balanced man, whose command over the ship is symbolic of the inner strength and self-command which knowledge of the shadow brings.[12] Thus, what Kirk and the viewing audience both learn in this program (which, like so many of the "Star Trek" episodes, is unabashedly didactic) is the need for staying in touch with "the enemy within," for maintaining a close connection with the "wild, untamed instinctuality" which is embodied in the primitive shadow and which—however repugnant this part of the personality may seem—is nevertheless the source of civilized man's vitality.

A similar lesson is learned by Ged, the young hero of Ursula K. Le Guin's novel *A Wizard of Earthsea*. This book, the first of Le Guin's "Earthsea Trilogy," is a work of "sword-and-sorcery" fantasy, a genre with close affinities to science fiction but with one very significant difference: whereas technology is the force that dominates the world of S-F, the power which rules in fantasy fiction is magic. Thus Ged, the apprentice wizard of Le Guin's novel, is rent in two, not by a malfunctioning machine, but by a bit of adolescent bravado: a dangerous "spell of Summoning" he weaves before having achieved full mastery over the magical arts.

Challenged by a hated rival to prove his skill, Ged arrogantly announces that he can perform the perilous deed of calling forth the dead, but when he tries to conjure up the spirit of the legendary lady Elfarrin, he accidentally unleashes a terrible power: a "foul cruel thing,"[13] an embodiment of pure evil, that pursues the young hero across the world in an attempt to enter and possess him—"to take his strength into itself, and suck up his life, and clothe itself in his flesh" (183). "You have great power inborn in you," says the Archmage Gensher to Ged after the boy has recovered from the first onslaught of the "shadow-beast" he has "raised up into the sunlight." But, the Archmage admonishes the boy, "you used that power wrongly, to work a spell over which you have no control, not knowing how that spell affects the balance of light and dark, life and death, good and evil." The beast "is the shadow of your arrogance, the shadow of your ignorance, the shadow you cast. Has a shadow a name?"

It is only by learning the name of the shadow-creature that the hero can hope to master it. After fleeing from it for years, Ged finally turns to confront his hideous foe by reaching out his hands toward it, and taking "hold of his shadow, of the black self that reached out to him." "Aloud and clearly...Ged spoke the shadow's name and in the same moment the shadow spoke without lips or tongue, saying the same word: 'Ged.' And the two voices were one voice" (178-79).

Like his literary forbear, Shakespeare's wizard Prospero, Ged acknowledges the "thing of darkness" as his own—an act of great courage and wisdom, indicative of Ged's spiritual maturation, of his development from a cocky and callow adolescent into a man who comes to know the deepest recesses of the self and thus achieves tremendous power. By "naming the shadow...with his own name," writes Le Guin, Ged "had made himself whole: a man: who, knowing his whole true self, cannot be used or possessed by any power other than himself, and whose life therefore is lived for life's sake and never in the service of ruin, or pain, or hatred, or the dark" (181).

Another popular culture figure analogous to Prospero, however, does not fare as well as Ged. Loosely modelled on *The Tempest,* the famous science fiction film of the 1950s, *Forbidden Planet,* concerns a space expedition from earth which lands on the arid planet Altair-4 and discovers a marooned scientist named Morbius, who lives alone with his daughter Altaira (the counterpart of Miranda) and a helpful robot called Robby—the mechanical equivalent of the sprite Ariel. Though Morbius has used the highly advanced technology of an extinct alien race called the Krell to create an Edenic abode for himself and his daughter, the visitors soon discover that there is a terrifyingly destructive creature at large on the planet: a black, formless thing that attacks them with demonic fury. What the earthmen and the audience eventually learn is that Morbius, in experimenting with the Krell machinery, has unleashed a living embodiment of his own most primitive impulses: a "monster from the id." Unlike his Shakespearean prototype, however, the scientist lacks the wisdom to come to terms with the hateful thing that is the expression of his own repressed rage. He tries to undo the damage he has caused by repudiating the creature, and is destroyed in the act of denying it.

What *Forbidden Planet* serves to illustrate, then, is that some works of popular art teach their psychological lesson by portraying not the positive effects of accepting the shadow but the disastrous results of disavowing it. The prototype of this kind of story is Robert Louis Stevenson's *The Strange Case of Dr. Jekyll and Mr. Hyde*, of which several different movie versions have been made, and which has inspired countless low-budget horror films about mad physicians or research scientists who concoct chemical potions which convert them into monsters. The catastrophic ending of Stevenson's tale—the terrible destruction of his essentially well-meaning hero—is symbolic of the psychological damage that is caused by a steadfast refusal to accept the shadow as a part of one's personality.

It is not that Henry Jekyll is ignorant of his shadow. On the contrary, he clearly recognizes his pleasure-seeking side. But he regards it as so immoral that he cannot reconcile it with his ideal image of himself as a dignified and dedicated man of the mind. For Jekyll, intellect and instinct are utterly incompatible aspects of human nature, and he does everything he can to sever the two halves of himself. If the "polar twins" he perceives in himself "could be housed in separate identities," he reasons, "life would relieve itself of all that was unbearable; the unjust might go his way, delivered from the aspirations and remorse of his more upright twin; and the just could walk steadfastly and securely on his upward path, doing the good things in which he found his pleasure, and no longer exposed to disgrace and penitence by the hands of this extraneous evil."[14] Jekyll's inability to live with so vital a part of himself—his perception of his (completely normal) appetites as base and degraded—inevitably leads to psychic disaster; for his fierce attempts at self-renunciation only make the demands of his shadow grow more and more intense, until he is utterly overwhelmed by them, annihilated by the monster who is the product of his own rigid and repressive morality.

Though the "Jekyll-and-Hyde theme," involving the conflict between the dissociated halves of a single personality, is a very common pattern in popular art, it is not the only way in which the struggle between civilized consciousness and its primitive shadow side is portrayed. Another recurrent motif is the battle between the "hostile brothers." "What was originally the cosmic opposition of light and darkness," writes the Jungian critic Alex

Aronson, "becomes, first, the conflict between the divine twin brothers and, later on, was reflected in countless folktales describing...the personalized conflict between the 'good' and 'evil' brothers, exemplified best in the biblical story of Cain and Abel."[15]

A good example of this motif can be seen in the cowboy movie *Duel in the Sun*. Released in 1947, and one of the top-grossing Westerns of all time, this film stars Joseph Cotten and Gregory Peck as the antagonistic McCanles brothers, Jesse and Lewt. Jesse—blonde, well-bred, benevolent—is a spokesman for societal values: for law, order, decency. He supports the coming of the railroad (though its tracks will cut across his father's ranch), believing that it will promote the development of Texas and bring civilization to the West. Ultimately, he becomes a lawyer and moves to the city.

Lewt, on the other hand, is an agent of *dis*order, the opposite of his brother in every way. Whereas Jesse is always attired in neat, brightly colored outfits and drives rather primly to town in a buckboard, Lewt wears dark, rugged work clothes and gallops bareback across the prairie on a high-spirited pinto pony. And whereas Jesse is their mother's favorite, Lewt is their father's. Violent, passionate, reckless, he becomes a fugitive after killing a cowhand who intends to marry Pearl Chavez—Lewt's spurned mistress—and turns to blowing up trains as a way of helping out his father. Finally, infuriated that Jessie and his wife have taken the outcast Pearl into their household, he guns his unarmed brother down in cold blood (only to be shot himself soon afterwards by his fiery former mistress).

Once again—in this work as in *Dr. Jekyll and Mr. Hyde*—the necessity of integrating the shadow is conveyed by showing the catastrophic effects of rejecting it. Jesse, the perfect gentleman, feels nothing but contempt for his "barbaric" brother; but no integration is possible so long as civilized consciousness cannot see anything worthwhile in instinctual behavior. Certainly the audience is allowed—even encouraged—to respond to Lewt's positive qualities, for, though the character is rotten to the core, his high animal spirits make him more attractive in many ways than his citified, almost sissified, older brother.

Popular culture, in fact, frequently portrays shadow figures who possess an appealing vitality that conventional "good guys" lack. In Garry Cleveland Myers' "Goofus and Gallant," for example, a regular feature of the monthly magazine *Highlights for Children,* the motif of the wicked brother is used in the service of moral instruction—to promote proper conduct in its young readers. Gallant is the ego ideal: a little paragon, everthing a nice, obedient boy should be. Goofus, on the other hand, is a typical shadow figure, embodying all the asocial tendencies that children are supposed to reject (fig. 1). But, though Goofus is clearly meant to be obnoxious, even destructive—a bundle of unbridled aggression—he generally seems more appealing than the do-gooder Gallant, a fact which the author himself seems to recognize. Concerned, apparently, that his readers might miss the point and emulate the wrong brother, Myers includes a little explanatory note on the bottom of each page stressing that "Gallant shows correct behavior."[16]

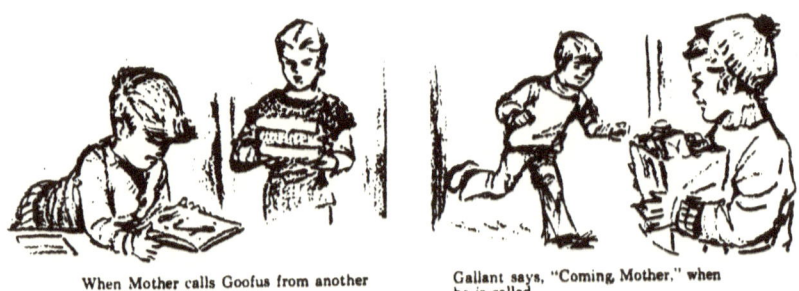

When Mother calls Goofus from another room he doesn't answer.

Gallant says, "Coming, Mother," when he is called.

Reprinted with permission from *Highlights for Children,* Columbus, Ohio, for *Goofus and Gallant,* copyright 1973.

The true hero of popular culture, then, is neither the goody-goody Gallant-Jesse type, nor the wild, if engaging Goofus-Lewt, but the character who represents an ideal integration of the civilized and the primitive, ego and shadow. Such heroes abound in popular art. Tarzan, who combines the savagery of a killer ape with the intelligence and refined sensibility of an English lord, is a prime example. Others include the Western hero, in his countless incarnations, who is both smarter and deadlier than the villains he fights; and the costumed superheroes of the comics like Captain Marvel—who, as we have seen, unites the wisdom of Solomon with the strength of Hercules—and his predecessor Superman, who can both outthink a computer and, with a flick of his little finger, send an opponent crashing through a brick wall. Though Clark Kent is Superman's alter-ego, the mild-mannered reporter does not represent the Man of Steel's shadow side; rather, Clark is a caricature of the modern urban man whose highly developed rationality (signified by his lack of physical coordination and his glasses) is, as Jung puts it, "won at the expense of his vitality."[17] Superman is the wish-fulfillment fantasy of the curbed and frustrated citydweller yearning to strip off his clothes and soar.

This kind of character—the contemporary personification of civilization and its discontents—is often found in the popular arts, where he is generally shown to be on some kind of real or imaginery quest for instinctual fulfillment. One of the most psychologically astute representations of this theme is Robert Crumb's story "Whiteman" from the "underground" comic book *Zap* (no. 1).[18]

As the subtitle informs us, "Whiteman" is "A Story of Civilization in Crisis." Its protagonist—the prototypical American businessman—"is on the verge of a nervous breakdown." Having struggled for years to make it in the big city (he likes to think of himself as "A real hard charger! The man with the know-how! A citizen on the go!"), he has become divorced from his "real self deep down inside," and is finding it increasingly difficult to control his "forbidden passions," his "illicit desires." The instinctual part of himself which he has denied for so long—"the raging lustful beast within"—now threatens to rise up and overwhelm him, and it is only through the greatest effort that he manages to keep it in check: "I must maintain this rigid position or all is lost!" But as Jungian analyst Liliane Frey-Rohn writes, "the deeper the repression, the more active the dissociated content"[19]—and Whiteman is finally forced to confront the dark, hidden side of his psyche.

Walking home from work one evening, he encounters a parade of black men—archetypal shadow figures, symbols of the white man's unconscious. Face to face for the first time with their shadows, most people respond with dread and denial—and Whiteman is no exception. Trembling in fear, he turns and runs from the blacks, but there is no escape. They chase after him, tear off his pants, and, as he cowers on the ground, point accusing fingers at him. "You jis' a nigger like eva body else," they tell him. "C'mon nigger! Yo' got music in yo' soul! Remember?" Then they run off, inviting him to join their parade (fig. 2). As Jung

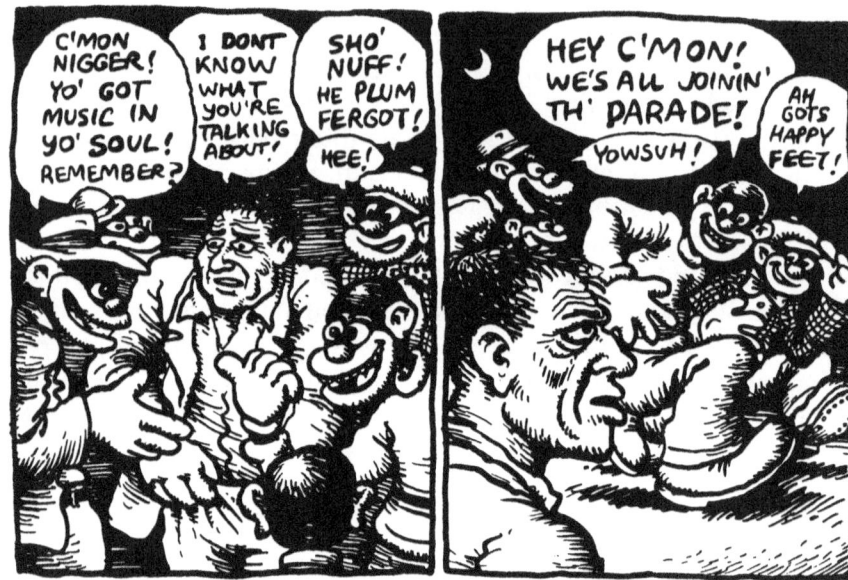

Reprinted with permission from R. Crumb for panels from "Whiteman."

emphasizes, the shadow is "not wholly bad," since it contains primitive energies which can "vitalize and embellish human existence."[20] By joining the parade, Whiteman would be recognizing "the validity of the primitive, which civilization represses."[21] At the end of the story, he is still putting up a good deal of resistance to the impulses embodied in his shadow—"Foolish nonsense...low class...What's the world coming to?" But Crumb at least holds out the hope that, someday, Whiteman will be able to accept those "inadmissable" impulses and achieve a psychic rebirth: "Will Whiteman join the parade?...Oh, eventually!"

The meeting with the shadow is clearly portrayed in another of Crumb's stories, "Sky-Hi Comics," a kind of abbreviated version of "Whiteman."[22] Bill Ding, a conservative and (quite literally) square white-collar type is strolling along the city streets, counting his salary, when three tiny figures—a light bulb, a radio dial and a drop of liquid—fall from the sky and break into a song-and-dance routine. "Come on and turn on, tune in, and dro-ho-hop out—that's what you gotta do!" they sing. Bill does not take kindly to their message, stomping the little characters to smithereens.

But later that night, stood up by his date and "broken hearted again," he admits that he is "sick of this rat race." As he plods home, bottle in hand, he is suddenly greeted by "a wild man"—a caricature cannibal in grass skirt and bone necklace. Bill is frightened at first, but the black reassures him: "Don't be scared! Gimme some skin baby!" The last panel shows Bill—with his suit, striped tie, and buttoned-down collar—happily shaking hands with the half-naked savage. "It's nevah too late," says the wild man. "So come on along! Yowsuh!" Having accepted the shadow, Bill can look forward to a revitalized existence: "This is the beginning of a new life for me!" (fig. 3).

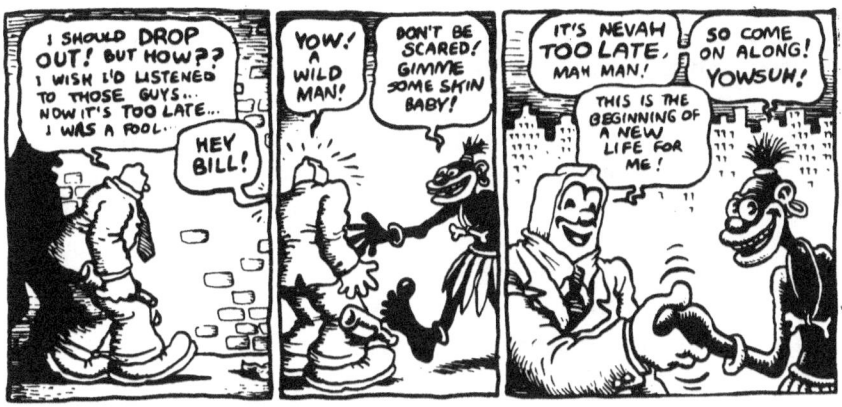

Reprinted with permission from R.C. Crumb from "Whiteman."

The friendship between two men of different races is an archetypal symbol of psychic integration, of the union of ego and shadow. It is especially common in classic American literature, where it is found in such works as Cooper's Leatherstocking Tales, Poe's *Narrative of A. Gordon Pym,* Melville's *Moby-Dick,* Mark Twain's *Adventures of Huckleberry Finn* and others. Leslie Fiedler has written eloquently and at length about the motif of "the idyllic and sexless union of a white man and a colored one."[23] He calls this recurrent theme the Myth of the Good Companion, and sees it as a dream-image of social and psychological harmony which haunts the American imagination. Several other critics, working from a Jungian perspective, have analyzed the psychological meaning of this motif, particularly as it appears in *Moby-Dick.*

This Myth of the Good Companion is similarly prevalent in American popular art, especially in Westerns, where it generally takes the form of a friendship between a glamorous white cowboy hero and his faithful Indian sidekick. The pair epitomizing this myth in popular culture is the Lone Ranger and Tonto, though countless other examples exist, including that caricature of the heroic Western couple, Joe Buck and Ratso Rizzo of *Midnight Cowboy*. (Ratso, of course, is neither a black man nor an Indian; nevertheless, being dark, foreign and entirely disreputable—a denison of the sleazy Times Square underworld—he serves as the perfect shadow figure for the blond, baby-faced naif, Joe.)

While the friendship with the shadow figure is a traditional symbol for psychic integration, there is another which, in the paradoxical way of unconscious imagery, takes a diametrically opposite form, though its meaning is ultimately the same. This is the mythic motif that Richard Slotkin calls "regeneration through violence,"[24] involving heroes who are "redeemed" not, like Ishmael, by embracing their "dark brothers" but by slaying them—who come together with their shadows not in love but in violence, thereby discovering in themselves a previously unsuspected level of primitive response.

This too, as Slotkin shows, is a powerful theme in our culture. In our fiction, it can be found at least as far back as 1799, in *Edgar Huntly, or Memoirs of a Sleepwalker,* by Charles Brockden Brown, "The Father of the American Novel." The hero of this book is a virtuous and cultivated young man, who is completely dedicated to the ideals of the Enlightenment. He believes that reason is "an antidote to the illusions of insanity," bears a powerful "antipathy to scenes of violence and bloodshed," and loftily proclaims that he has "ever aspired to transcend the rest of animals in all that is common to the rational and brute, as well as in all by which they are distinguished from each other."[25] He is, in short, a preeminently civilized being, a true product of the Age of Reason.

Nevertheless, at one point in the novel, Edgar, lost in the wilderness and dying of thirst, finds his path to a nearby stream blocked by a ferocious Mohawk brave. Edgar is reluctant to "imbrue [his] hands in the blood" of this Indian (170), but he is "assailed by the torments of thirst" (161); and so, overcoming his "aversion to bloodshed" (169), he buries a hatchet in the Indian's breast. By slaying this "savage," Edgar becomes a savage himself—i.e., assimilates the spirit of the wilderness into his conscious personality—and as a result, experiences a profound sense of renewal. For as soon as the Indian falls, Huntly rushes to the stream and plunges in—an archetypal symbol of rebirth. "Never was any delight worthy of comparison with the raptures which I then experienced," he cries. "My languors...vanished in a moment, and I felt prepared to undergo the labors of Hercules" (172). For the civilized man separated from the instinctual roots of his being, such an upsurge of energy is precisely the effect which the realization of the shadow will produce.

Popular art is full of characters like Edgar Huntly: decent, law-abiding men whose civilized self-restraint places them in situations of physical peril—a theme which symbolizes the psychological dangers of extreme repression, of cutting oneself off too completely from the shadow.

The comic book story "Midnight Brings Dark Death" is an interesting example.[26] In it, the shadow figure appears in the archetypal form of the hostile brother. Shang-chi, the noble Chinese-American hero, has become the sworn enemy of his father, the Oriental arch-fiend Fu Manchu, whose diabolical nature has only lately been disclosed to the young man. Fu Manchu in turn attempts to dispose of his son by forcing him into a deadly duel with "the man-menace called Midnight": Shang-chi's evil foster brother, whose real name is M'nai. Here, once again, the shadow figure is a black man—a horribly scarred African who hides his deformity behind a sable cowl. In fact, Midnight's combat outfit is entirely black, flat black, so that in the fight scenes, Shang-chi appears to be engaged in a particularly lethal form of shadow-boxing, as if his shadow had suddenly developed a will of its own and turned on him with murderous intent (fig. 4).

As the two men battle fiercely, Shang-chi—though he is a master of the martial arts—finds himself on the defensive, fleeing from the ferocious M'nai. Cornered by his dark brother, the hero appears to be on the brink of destruction, when he has a sudden, saving insight:

...a new understanding of myself opens before me! I accepted the inevitability of the battle—accepted the battle itself—but I never truly accepted the death at the battle's end! I said I did—thought I did—but the concept of actually killing M'nai remained only a concept, not a possibility! I have never felt the death-power in my limbs tonight! I have struck to injure, to disable—but never to destroy!

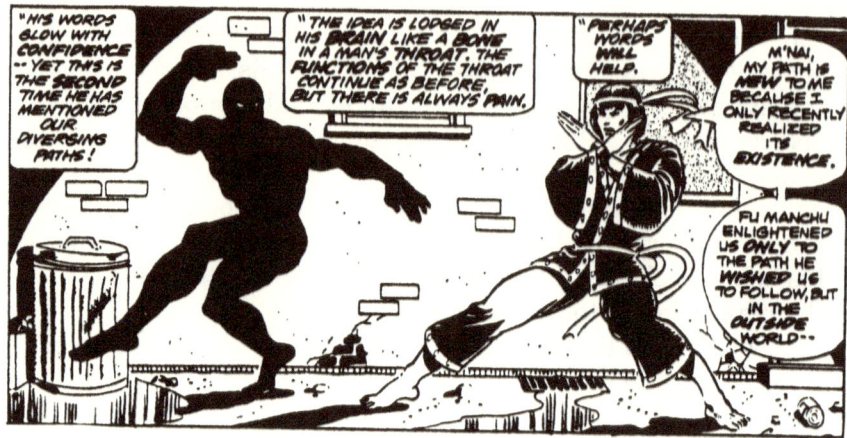

Reprinted with permission from Marvel Comics for panel art from "Midnight Brings Dark Death", *Master Kung Fu*, copyright ⸢ 1974.

As soon as he recognizes this truth, Shang-chi is able to defeat his evil brother. It is only by accepting his "death-power," then, his full capacity for violence and destruction—only, that is to say, by "realizing his shadow" and becoming a "man-menace" himself— that the young hero is saved.

Because the theme of "regeneration through violence" involves heroes who are revitalized or reborn through the act of slaying their adversaries, its meaning is often misunderstood. Two popular works which deal with this theme—Sam Peckinpah's controversial movie *Straw Dogs* and James Dickey's bestselling novel *Deliverance*—have both been subject to such misunderstanding.

Peckinpah's film centers on a mild-mannered math professor from Boston, David Sumner (played by Dustin Hoffman). While spending his sabbatical year in his wife's native village in Cornwall, Sumner is forced to defend his woman and his home against a bunch of barbarous locals who, in their violence and carnality, serve as symbols of man's dark, uncivilizable side. At the end of the movie, Sumner manages to kill all his tormentors, and, as a result, he achieves not only physical salvation but psychic renewal: he feels better, more *alive,* than he has ever felt before.

Critics and viewers alike condemned the presumed message of the movie: that the achievement of manhood "requires rites of violence, that home and hearth are inviolate and must be defended by blood, that a man must conquer other men to prove his courage and hold on to his woman," and that intellectuals are "less than real men" because they are "distanced by their sedentary lives from the essential functions of fighting and fornicating."[27] It seems to me, however, that such a reading takes the action of what is essentially a Gothic work too literally. What the movie tells us in symbolic terms, I believe, is not that one must shed blood in order to become a "real man," but that in order to become fully human we must recognize our inherent animality: not deny or repress it but accept it as a vital part of our nature.

A similar meaning informs James Dickey's *Deliverance*—a work I propose to analyze in detail in the following section. Dickey's bestseller is worth examining closely because it operates so well on two separate levels: first, on the literal level, as a fast-paced and gripping adventure story, and, second, on the symbolic, as an extremely astute portrayal of the individuation process—of a discontented, middle-aged man whose quest for fulfillment leads him toward an archteypal confrontation with the shadow.

2

Deliverance opens with a pair of epigraphs, one describing the narrator's problem, the second suggesting a solution. The first, from Georges Bataille, says, *"Il existe à base de la vie humaine un principe d'insuffisance"*—"There exists at the base of human life an element of incompleteness." That Ed Gentry, the hero of Dickey's novel, is indeed feeling that his life lacks something essential is made very clear in the beginning section of the book. This prologue to the main action, entitled "Before,"[28] introduces us to a character suffering from that malaise which, according to Jungian psychologists, commonly afflicts men and women during the second half of life—that depression which descends upon "middle-aged people who, having been successful in their chosen career, suddenly awake to a feeling of emptiness and lack of meaning in their lives."[29] "We had grooved as a studio" (16), he thinks, referring to the thriving advertising agency he runs with his partner, Thad Emerson. "We had made it what it was; we had made it" (23).

But as he walks back to his office from a lunch date with some friends, this "middle-aged responsible" man—"Vice-President

Gentry" (18)—is suddenly hit by a deep sense of his own mortality: "Going under a heavy shade tree, I felt the beer come up, not into my throat but into my eyes. The day sparkled painfully, seeming to shake on some kind of axis, and through this a leaf fell, touched with unusual color at the edge. It was the first time I had realized that autumn was close. I began to climb the last hill," he says significantly (a little too significantly; Dickey is usually a good deal more deft in his handling of symbols). Inside his office, Gentry is again overcome by "the old mortal, helpless, time-terrified human feeling": "The feeling of the inconsequence of whatever I would do, of anything I would pick up or think about or turn to see was at that moment being set in the very bone marrow. How does one get through this? I asked myself" (19). "It all seemed like everything just went right by me, nothing mattered at all" (29).

Gentry, it is clear, is going through what is commonly called, in these days of pop psychology, a "mid-life crisis." All the classic symptoms are there: the feeling of being trapped ("I was not really thinking about their being my prisoners," he says at one point, referring to his employees, "but of being my own"[18], and the restlessness that accompanies, it; the sense that, though he has won all the right prizes—the station wagon, the house in the suburbs, the color TV—his life adds up to nothing, that it is rich in material possessions but empty of meaning.

He has a sexual infatuation with a model half his age and a marriage which, though decent and loving, no longer holds much excitement for him (in an early lovemaking scene with his wife, Martha, it is she who takes the active role, manipulates and issues commands, while Ed remains passive and detached, dreaming of the model and commenting on his wife's "practical approach to sex" [29]). Everything about his life seems sterile and unfulfilling to him. Though he works as the art director of his ad agency, for instance, he does not consider himself to be at all creative: "[My wife] insisted on believing that I had talent as an artist though I had none. I was a mechanic of the graphic arts, and when I could get the problem to appear mechanical to me, and not the result of inspiration, I could do something with it" (28).

This sense of emptiness, meaninglessness, psychic sterility is, Jungians tell us, the result of the one-sided psychological development that social adaptation demands—the necessity for sharpening consciousness while repressing one's instinctive nature. Ed Gentry is a prime example of the civilized man who has become dangerously dissociated from his instinctual self, from the primitive energies of the psyche which society forces us to deny. Images evoking the tension between nature and culture abound in the book: a view of the trees in Ed's back yard, "wild, free things...in a domestic setting" (33); a vision of "domestic animals suddenly turning and crushing one against the splintering side of a barn stall" (52); a quick glimpse of the primitive forces "moiling" beneath the tidy surface of a happy suburban household, as Ed's son Dean "playfully" stalks his father with a sheathed Bowie knife after father and mother have made love, and Ed suddenly grows conscious of the vulnerability of his naked genitals beneath his bathrobe.[30] All these things— along with the repeated references to the "monkey fur" on Ed's body, the vestigial mark of his animal ancestry—are symbols of the narrator's plight, of his deeply felt distance from the instinctual roots of his being.

What is the answer to this problem? As I said earlier, it seems to me that the solution is suggested by the second epigraph which Dickey prefixes to his story: "The pride of thine heart hath deceived thee, thou that dwellest in the clefts of the rock, whose habitation is high; that saith in his heart, Who shall bring me down to the ground?" (*Obadiah,* verse 3). While some critics have read this as an allusion to the mountain men who figure in the story ("thou that dwellest in the clefts of the rock"), it makes more sense to me as a reference to Ed, the upper middle class city dweller, a member of the "gentry" (as his name suggests),[31] who must, in order to be cured of his complaint, be "brought down to the ground"—made aware of an important connection to the natural world. Read in this way, the epigraph applies not only to the external action of the story—the "back-to-nature" plot—but also to its psychological action. In psychological terms, the epigraph may be taken to refer to a consciousness which has become too highly developed and must be put back in touch with the "lowly" instinctual level of the psyche from which it has become detached.

How can such a reattachment be achieved? Reestablishing a connection between the various parts of the psyche is precisely the goal of analytical psychology, and is accomplished, as we have seen, by means of the individuation process, which acts "to abolish the separation between the conscious mind and the unconscious, the real source of life, and to bring about a reunion of the individual with the native soil of his inherited, instinctual make-up."[32] And this psychological process is, I believe, precisely what *Deliverance* portrays. Dickey's novel, that is to say, is essentially a visionary work which depicts the quest for self-realization and the confrontation with the alien powers of the deep unconscious.

"In dreams or myths," writes the Jungian analyst Joseph Henderson, "individuation most frequently presents itself as the lively, urgent wish to undertake a journey"[33]—and in the opening section of *Deliverance*, Dickey introduces us to four Southern suburbanites planning a week-end canoe trip into the backwoods of Georgia. Ed himself expresses a "lively" desire to go—"I...felt ready for something like this" (8)—but the urgency is communicated more by his companion Lewis Medlock, who, playing the role of the mythological "herald," announces his determination to travel down the "wild rippling water" (36) before the river is dammed and the Cahulawasee is transformed into Lake Cahula, a "real estate heaven" of "choice lots...marinas and beer cans" (7). The other two members of the group, Bobby Trippe and Drew Ballinger, have reservations about the journey, don't feel any particular need for it. "The whole thing does seem kind of crazy," Bobby says (10). But, like Ahab on the quarter-deck, Lewis goads them on.

There are, as a matter of fact, interesting similarities between *Deliverance* and *Moby-Dick*. In many ways, Drew is just like Starbuck. Staid and steadfast, domestic and devout—"The only decent one; the only sane one" (186)—he is incapacitated by his own normalcy: a man whose "mere unaided virtue or right-mindedness" affords him no protection against "spiritual terrors" and who is inevitably destroyed by the voyage to Hades.[34]

Bobby, on the other hand, resembles Stubb, the typical Melvillean bachelor, jolly and obtuse—the clown who can journey into the heart of darkness without understanding anything at all about the experience; whose smug satisfaction with the world is a sign of his spiritual shallowness:

...Bobby, particularly, seemed to enjoy the life he was in. He came, I believe, from

some other part of the South, maybe Louisiana, and since he had been around—
since I had known him, anyway—had seemed to do well. He was very social and
would not have been displeased if someone had called him a born salesman. He
liked people, he said, and most of them liked him—some genuinely and some
merely because he was a bachelor and a good dinner or party guest.... He was a
pleasant surface human being (11).

Lewis, the leader of the expedition, is, as I have suggested,
similar to Ahab. Driven, obsessed (12), fanatical (40), "insane"
(230), he sees the canoe trip, not simply as a weekend jaunt, but "A
Way"—a quest for immortality:

Lewis wanted to be immortal. He had everything that life could give, and he
couldn't make it work. And couldn't bear to give it up or see age take it away from
him, either, because in the meantime he might be able to find what it was he
wanted, the thing that must be there, and that must be subject to the will. He was
the kind of man who tries by any means—weight lifting, diet, exercise...—to hold
on to his body...to rise above time (12).

Lewis, I believe, is suffering from a neurotically extreme fear of
dying. This may seen an odd assertion, given his compulsive
daredeviltry. But after all, neurotic phobias often express
themselves in paradoxical ways, so that a person suffering from a
pathological fear of speed, for instance, may never set foot in a car
or, alternatively, may become a professional racer. The two
responses are just flip sides of a single coin. Lewis' craving for
immortality is simply a desperate desire not to die. At the same
time, as Ed himself is well aware, Lewis' accident-proneness
reveals an equally desperate desire *to* die, as if he is eager to
relieve himself of the burden of his terrible fear (12). After
fracturing his thigh in the rapids, however, Lewis finally comes
to "know something that I didn't know before" (194)—"that dying
is better than immortality" (235). No longer compelled to play
superman, he becomes "a human being, and a good one" (235), at
peace with himself at last. Thus, though he and Ahab both suffer
crippling leg injuries—"It feels like it broke off," Lewis gasps
(126)—the significance of the wound is very different for each
man: for Lewis, it means the end of his quest, for Ahab the
beginning.

Like Ishmael, who is carried away with the rest of the crew by
the "irresistible arm" of Ahab's rhetoric, Ed listens to his friend
and feels himself "getting caught up...in his capricious and

tenacious enthusiasm" (9). For Gentry, the canoe trip is also "a Way," though not to physical fitness. Whereas Lewis regards the Georgia wilderness as a testing-ground for his body, Ed looks at a map of the area and sees something else: "It was certainly not much from the standpoint of design. The high ground, in tan and an even paler tone of brown, meandered in and out of various shades of green, and there was nothing to call you or stop you on one place or another. Yet the eye could not leave the whole; there was harmony of some kind" (13).

Right from the start, the region of the unknown holds out the promise of spiritual wholeness, psychic serenity, self-realization, to Gentry. Just as the narrator of *Moby-Dick* must leave the "insular city of the Manhattoes" and travel into "the mystic ocean," "the dark side of the earth," to cure his spiritual sickness—the "damp, drizzly November" in his soul[35]—the narrator of *Deliverance* is impelled to journey into night country in order to dispel *his* hypos. Like the schoolteacher Ishmael, whose spiritual quest unites him with the neglected instinctual side of his psyche, embodied by the cannibal Queequeg, Gentry must make the inner voyage to confront those primitive qualities which, when assimilated, will revitalize his existence.

As he sets out for the valley, Ed expresses some skepticism about the trip. He defends "the way of civilization," of order and comfort and rationality, while Lewis extols nature and asserts that city life is "out of touch with everything" (42). "You don't believe in madness, eh?" asks Medlock.

"I don't at all. I know better than to fool with it."
"So what you do...."
"So what you do is go on by it. What you do is get done what you ought to be doing. And what you do rarely—and I *mean* rarely—is to flirt with it."
"We'll see," Lewis said, glancing at me as though he had me. "We'll see. You've had all that office furniture in front of you, desks and bookcases and filing cabinets and the rest. You've been sitting in a chair that won't move. You've been steady. But when that river is under you, all that is going to change" (40)

Ed's reservations about the wilderness experience—"I'll still stay with the city," he insists (46)—reflect the conscious mind's natural resistance to entering the realm of the irrational. But, as all heroes must, Ed responds to the "call" of the unconscious and takes the plunge. That his journey is indeed a dream trip—a symbol of the descent into the darkness of the unconscious—becomes clear as soon as he enters the river: "A slow force took hold of us; the bank began to go backward. I felt the complicated urgency of the current, like a thing made of many threads being pulled, and with this came the feeling I always had at the moment of losing consciousness at night, going towards something unknown that I could not avoid, but from which I would return" (65-66).

As Gentry travels farther into the woods, he begins to make contact with the alien forces of his psyche—a situation symbolized by a dreamlike experience he has on the first night of the journey. Lying in the blackness of his tent, deep in the forest, he is startled when something slams against the roof. He snaps on a flashlight and runs "the weak glow up from the door...."

I kept seeing nothing but gray-green stitches until I got right above my head. The canvas was punctured there, and through it came one knuckle of a deformed fist, a long curving of claws that turned on themselves. Those are called talons, I said out loud.

*   *   *

I pulled one hand out of the sleeping bag and saw it wander frailly up through the thin light until a finger touched the cold reptilian nail of one talon below the leg-scales. I had no idea of whether the owl felt me; I thought perhaps it would fly, but it didn't. Instead it shifted its weight again, and the claws on the foot I was touching loosened for a second. I slipped my forefinger between the claw and the tent, and half around the stony toe (78).

This strange, hallucinatory scene represents, as Donald W. Markos points out, "the penetration of the wilderness into human consciousness"[36]—i.e., the breakdown of the barrier between the ego and the unconscious. The owl, a creature associated with night vision and wisdom, symbolizes Ed's increasing insight into the darkness of his psyche.

In a perceptive essay on *Deliverance,* Donald J. Greiner discusses the book in terms of Ed's growing self-knowledge, and maintains that Dickey's central concern is bestiality: "In *Deliverance* Dickey goes beyond the violent action and he-man acrobatics to suggest that each of us harbors in the deepest recesses of himself an unknown part which we are afraid to face because we might be forced to acknowledge our own bestiality." The narrator's spiritual development, Greiner argues, depends precisely on his ability to accept that "unknown part," to "call

forth the monster within...to meet [his buried self] face to face."
"The adventure in the big woods teaches [Ed] ...that self-
awareness means an acknowledgement of and harmonious
relationship between the two sides of his nature, the bestial and
the human."[37] Though Greiner's approach is not Jungian, his
insights correspond very closely to archetypal theory. For as we
have seen, self-realization, according to Jung, invariably begins
with the recognition of the shadow, the meeting with the
"monster within."

In *Deliverance* that meeting takes place early in the second
day of the trip, when, "in the intense shadow" of the woods (98),
Ed and Bobby encounter a pair of grotesque mountaineers:

> They came forward, moving in a kind of half circle as though they were stepping
> around something. The shorter one was older, with big white eyes and a half-white
> stubble that grew in whorls on his cheeks. His face seemed to spin in many
> directions. He had on overalls, and his stomach looked like it was falling through
> them. The other was lean and tall, and peered at us as though out of a cave or some
> dim simple place far back in his yellow-tinged eyeballs (95).

For Gentry, this second man is indeed "the Other"—the
Enemy, the Hostile Brother: that figure who represents the
hidden side of Ed's personality, "its lower, primitive, instinctual,
sensual half." Ignorant, incomprehensibly brutal (98), animal-
like (102), "repulsive-looking" (170), he is the personification of
the city man's "inadmissable" impulses—of sheer, unbridled
carnality and aggression. The utter bestiality of the
mountaineers——"Pull your shirt-tail up, fat ass" (99)—is the
antithesis of Ed's civilized behavior, of his sensitivity and rather
passive sexuality.

Confronted with the horror of his shadow's repellent urges,
Ed resists his insight at first, strives to reassert his rationality:
"The lean man put the point of the knife under my chin and lifted
it. 'You ever had your balls cut off, you fuckin' ape?' 'Not lately,' I
said, clinging to the city" (98). It soon becomes apparent,
however, that, if Ed is to survive, it will be necessary for him not
merely to face his shadow but to come to terms with it. In order to
be reborn, in order to achieve deliverance, Ed must become a
savage himself—i.e., incorporate the shadow archetype into his
conscious personality.

The process of accepting his inherent animality, of

acknowledging the primitive impulses which constitute the shadow, begins when the first mountaineer is slain and Ed approves Lewis' plan to bury the corpse in the woods. As the four men drag the body upstream, their civilized veneer is stripped away, and Gentry finds himself transformed into a beast: down on all fours in the "squelchy" muck, panting and digging wildly with his hands (117). Ed's metamorphosis is made explicit a few pages later when Drew is (apparently) shot in the head and the canoe overturns, spilling the narrator into the rapids: "I got on my back and poured with the river, sliding over the stones like a creature I had always contained but never released" (124). Attempting to right the canoe, he thinks of himself as "an out-of-shape animal" (127).

Here he is beginning to identify himself with his antagonist, who had leaped into the forest "like an animal" (102) when his partner was killed; an identification which signifies Ed's conscious realization of his shadow side, his recognition of a connection with the archetype. Indeed, as Ed crouches at the bottom of the gorge beside Lewis and Bobby, trying to figure out a way to save them all from the "murderous hillbilly" above (135), his "hidden" personality rises to consciousness and he experiences the Other within:

> "I think," I said, "that we'll never get out of this gorge alive."
> Did I say that? I thought. Yes, a dream-man said, you did. You did say it, and you believe it.
> "I think he means to pick the rest of us off tomorrow," I said out loud, *still stranger* than anything I had ever imagined.
>
>   *   *   *
>
> "What can we do?"
> "We can do three things," I said, and *some other person* began to tell me what they were (129-130; my italics).

Liliane Frey-Rohn, describing the emergence of the shadow into consciousness, writes that "In such cases one often has the impression that the psyche is being controlled by a 'stranger' who appears as a 'voice'...."[38] Ed has started to know his shadow, but it still remains an alien entity. His next task, difficult and extremely dangerous, is the full assimilation of the "inner opponent" of the "archetypal figure of the adversary."

Ed's perilous ascent of the cliff "as smooth as monument stone" (141) is a version of the archetypal trial—the fairy tale hero's climb up the crystal mountain to win "the treasure hard to attain." At one point, the experience becomes deeply erotic: desperately fighting for a handhold on the wall, Ed loses control of his bladder and his urine flows "with a delicious sexual voiding like a wet dream" (140). Suddenly the "immense rock...spring[s] a crack" and Ed crawls inside it, where he lies motionless "as though...in a sideways grave." "I simply lay in nature, my pants' legs warm and sopping with my juices" (145). This episode symbolizes Ed's penetration into the tomb-womb of the great Earth Mother and is an instance of what Jungians call "heroic" or "regenerative" incest: the act of entering into "the Mother"— the maternal unconscious—"in order to be reborn through her."[39]

That Ed's "heroic incest" with *Magna Mater* does indeed bring him closer to self-realization is indicated by the appearance, at this point in the novel, of the mandala symbol— the magic circle, an archetypal symbol of the Self. As he begins to "inch upward again," he finds himself "moving with the most intimate motions of my body, motions I had never dared use with Martha or with any other human woman. Fear and a kind of moon-blazing sexuality lifted me, millimeter by millimeter" (151). "Fuck[ing] the cliff for an extra inch or two in the moonlight," Ed suddenly sees some holes in the rocks above him, "and in one of them was a star....As I went, more stars were added until a constellation like a crown began to form" (151). This circle of light is a vision of wholeness, a prefiguration of the psychic totality which awaits him at the end of his ordeals. "The mountain," writes Marie-Louise Von Franz in her *Introduction to the Interpretation of Fairy Tales,* "marks the place...where the hero, after arduous effort (climbing), becomes oriented and gains steadfastness and self-knowledge, values that develop through the effort to become conscious in the process of individuation."[40]

Having conquered the mountain, Ed is finally prepared for the confrontation with the Enemy. His heroic "effort to become conscious" has brought him to the verge of a critical stage in the individuation process: the full realization of his shadow, of his own capacity for evil. "At a definite moment of time," writes Liliane Frey-Rohn, "the self seems to 'demand' that the personality be made complete through the recognition of what were up until then hostile, immoral and asocial tendencies."[41] This recognition, as I have suggested, is commonly symbolized by the slaying of the Adversary. "The 'hostile brother' has to be faced, overcome, incorporated into one's own psyche. Only in such a way can the ego evolve from partial self-knowledge to complete assimilation of the unconscious."[42]

Even before Ed kills his enemy, however, their coalescence is nearly complete: setting up an ambush for the mountaineer, the narrator feels "our minds fuse," and imagines himself performing fellatio on the stranger—visualizes a very literal act of incorporation. "If Lewis had not shot his companion, he and I would have made a kind of love, painful and terrifying to me, in some dreadful way pleasurable to him, but we would have been together in the flesh, there on the floor of the woods, and it was strange to think of it" (154). "A peculiar kind of intimacy" has developed between them (163), and when the mountaineer finally appears, he seems different from the utterly repulsive creature that had attacked Ed and Bobby in the forest: "He was looking up the river and standing now with both hands on the gun, but with the attitude of holding it at his waist without necessarily thinking of raising it to his shoulder. There was something relaxed and enjoying in his body position, something primally graceful; I had never seen a more beautiful element of design" (161).

Ed's shadow has suddenly assumed another aspect, positive and benign. "Unassimilated, the shadow figure [is entirely] evil," observes John Halverson, "a constellation of all that is demonic in the dark side of the psyche." As the archetype is integrated, however, the shadow begins to play a constructive role—"helping to bring up to consciousness those elements of the unconscious...necessary to the wholeness and health of the self"—and the stranger reveals himself to be the hero's helpmate and lover.[43]

The realization of the shadow is achieved with the mountaineer's death. Shooting a razor-sharp arrow through his adversary's throat, Ed becomes fully conscious of his capacity for violence. And when the wounded man crawls off, like an animal, to die in the bush, the narrator acknowledges his own bestiality by "getting down on my hands and knees and smelling for blood"—tracking his quarry "like a dog" (168, 169). When Gentry finally locates the corpse, he even considers cannibalizing it:

I took the knife in my fist. What? Anything. This, also, is not going to be seen. It is not ever going to be known; you can do what you want to; nothing is too terrible. I can cut off the genitals he was going to use on me. Or I can cut off his head, looking straight into his open eyes. Or I can eat him. I can do anything I have a wish to do....(170).

"The hero," says Joseph Campbell, "whether god or goddess, man or woman, the figure in a myth or the dreamer of a dream, discovers and assimilates his opposite (his own unsuspected self) either by swallowing it or by being swallowed."[44] While Ed does not commit "the ultimate horror," he *does* have the sensation of "being swallowed" by his shadow, momentarily possessed by his enemy's spirit. Walking "to the edge of the bluff" to see if Bobby has made good his escape, Ed spots the canoe on the river and— furious at Bobby for doing "everything wrong"—picks up the mountaineer's rifle and draws a bead on the "soft city country-club man." "Do it, the dead man said. Do it, he's right there" (171). The incident represents the surfacing of absolute evil in Ed, of the civilized man's most malevolent impulses. But he does not yield to these impulses: "I got around the feeling just by opening my fingers and letting the gun fall to the ground." While the narrator is now fully conscious of the existence of his shadow tendencies, he does not unconditionally surrender to them. Rather, he manages to integrate the two parts of his personality, the civilized and the bestial—succeeds, as Jung puts it, in joining the shadow to the light. This psychological condition is symbolized by the actual joining of Ed and the mountaineer: having lowered the dead man down the cliff on a nylon rope, Ed follows after him and, for a while, the two hang suspended in space, connected by a cord (a scene reminiscent of chapter 72 in *Moby-Dick,* where the relationship between Ishmael and Queequeg is symbolized by the "monkey-rope" which ties them together like "inseparable twin brother[s]).

When the cord suddenly snaps, Ed plunges headlong into the icy river:

I yelled, a tremendous, walled-in yell, and then I felt the current thread through me, first through my head from one ear and out the other and then complicatedly through my body, up my rectum and out my mouth and also in at the side where I was hurt....It had been so many years since I had really been hurt that the feeling was almost luxurious, though I knew when I tried to climb the water to the surface that I had been weakened more than I had thought. Unconsciousness went through me. I was in a room of varying shades of green beautifully graduated from light to dark, and I went toward the palest color. . . . An instant before I broke water I saw the sun, liquid and transformed, and then it exploded in my face (177).

The "black waters of death," writes Jung, are also "the water of life, for death with its cold embrace is the maternal womb just as the sea devours the sun but brings it forth again."[45] Having suffered this ritual death, Ed is finally prepared for his deliverance, and gradually makes his way out of the valley. His reintegration into society completes the mythic pattern which structures his story: separation-initiation-return. And his "trial by landscape" produces a striking transformation. Awakening in a boarding-house room on the morning after his return, Ed examines himself in a mirror and sees an "apparition" that bears little resemblance to the respectable suburbanite who had set out for the river a few days before. Stitched and bandaged, wearing a tattered flying suit with a web belt and a hunting knife, he looks like a wild man, a barbarian—"bearded and red eyed, not able to speak" (207).

This savage he sees in the mirror is, of course, his own "inmost part,"[46] the shadow side of his civilized consciousness. Having completed his night journey, Gentry now clearly recognizes the primitive aspect of his personality. More important, he is able to *accept* this side of himself: looking at his reflection, at the image of his violent inner self, Ed smiles "very whitely, splitting the beard" (207). By acknowledging the reality of his instinctual nature, Gentry wins the boon: the harmony he has been searching for.

That the experience in the wilderness does indeed benefit Ed by putting him in touch with an immanent power which enriches every aspect of his life is made very clear near the end of the novel:

Another odd thing happened. The river and everything I remembered about it became a possession to me, a private possession, as nothing in my life ever had. Now it ran nowhere but in my head, but there it ran as though immortally. I could feel it—I can feel it—on different places on my body. It pleases me in some curious way that the river does not exist, and that I have it. In me it still is, and will be until I die, green, rocky, deep, fast, slow, and beautiful beyond reality. I had a friend there who in a way had died for me, and my enemy was there.

The river underlies in one way or another everything I do. It is always finding a way to serve me, from my archery to some of my recent ads and to the new collages I have been attempting for my friends. George Holley, my old Braque enthusiast, bought one from me...and it hangs in his cubicle, full of sinuous forms threading among the headlines of war and student strikes. George has become my best friend, next to Lewis, and we do a lot of serious talking about art...(234).

This activation of Ed's imaginative powers—his metamorphosis from a "mechanic of the graphic arts" into a serious artist—is evidence of his new relation to what Frey-Rohn calls "the creative sources in the psyche." The adventure on the "night river" (235) has produced a significant enlargement of Ed's personality, an "inner transformation and rebirth into another being."[47] Revitalized and self-possessed, he relates more effectively, not only to the inner forces of his unconscious, but to the people around him as well. "Thad and I are getting along much better than before," he says, referring to his business partner, and George Holley, the "Braque man" who had seemed so tiresome to Gentry before the trip, is now the narrator's second-best friend. Thus, *Deliverance* portrays the dangers and rewards of the descent into the "land of impossibility" (235), into the dark, unknown depths of the psyche. "To sojourn in those depths," writes Jolande Jacobi, "to withstand their dangers, is a journey to hell and 'death.' But he who comes through safe and sound, who is 'reborn,' will return, full of knowledge and wisdom, equipped for the outward and inward demands of life."[48]

Chapter Three

Animal House:
Images of the Collective Shadow

IN HIS DISCUSSIONS of the shadow archetype, Jung draws a distinction between its personal and collective aspects. As we have seen, he defined the shadow, first of all, as a symbol of the personal unconscious, an embodiment of character traits "which appear morally, aesthetically, or intellectually inadmissable, and are repressed on account of their incompatibility."[1] When the shadow appears in an individual's dreams, therefore, it always represents those negative qualities, those shameful or hateful parts of his particular personality, which he would rather not know about—indeed, which he would probably vehemently deny possessing at all. The analytical psychologist Edward C. Whitmont gives the following example of the shadow archetype as it emerged in a dream produced by a patient of his who liked to think of himself as a "very liberal, tolerant, and broad-minded" person: "Coming home, I find that my apartment is occupied by a fascist who, with his militia, has turned everything upside down. He has arrested everybody in the house and put them in chains. The place is a shambles." According to Whitmont's interpretation, the fascist in this dream is the shadow self of the "progressive, broad-minded dreamer," who is notified here that there is "a totalitarian dictator in his house, that is, in his personality make-up....Our dreamer, of course, is a fascist-hater, in fact he will become very emotional and excited when the word is mentioned." Thus, the dream confronts the individual "with the very thing which he resents; it is presented as an integral part of his own personality and as one that may not be disregarded without danger." As we would expect, this "element is something which the dreamer is least willing to consider as part of his personality make-up."[2]

Besides representing repressed character traits, however, the shadow can also stand for a less individualized part of the personality, one which belongs to human nature in general. This impersonal side of the psyche—this "wild, untamed instinctuality" common to all people[3]—Jungians refer to as the *collective* shadow. Since the collective shadow corresponds to the most primitive, archaic level of the human mind—that level which links us with our animal past—it is often symbolized by a beast or some sort of anthropomorphized animal. The imaginative works of the world are rife with representations of this archetypal symbol, and in the present chapter I intend to examine two of its most important manifestations: the trickster and the helpful animal.

1

The trickster is one of mankind's oldest and most ubiquitous mythic figures. It is "found in clearly recognizable form among the simplest aboriginal tribes and the most complex," writes Paul Radin in *The Trickster,* his classic study of Winnebago Indian mythology. "We encounter it among the ancient Greeks, the Chinese, the Japanese, and in the Semitic world. Many of the Trickster's traits were perpetuated in the figure of the mediaeval jester, and have survived right up to the present day in the Punch-and-Judy plays and in the clown." It is clear, Radin concludes, that "we are here in the presence of a figure and a theme...which have had a special and permanent appeal and an unusual attraction for mankind from the very beginning of civilization."[4]

The most complete analysis of the meaning of this archetypal image can be found in Jung's essay "On the Psychology of the Trickster-Figure," included as a commentary at the end of Radin's volume. In this piece, Jung first describes the myriad manifestations of this symbol—its emergence "in picaresque tales, in carnivals and revels, in sacred and magical rites, in man's religious fears and exaltations"—and then attempts to provide a psychological explanation for its vitality, its enduring appeal.

Observing that the trickster seems to embody "an absolutely undifferentiated human consciousness, corresponding to a psyche that has hardly left the animal level," he asks how it is that this myth "has not long since vanished into the rubbish heap of the past, and why it continues to make its influence felt on the highest level of civilization." His conclusion is that the trickster myth has been "preserved and developed" for so long because of its "therapeutic effect." "What the repeated telling of the myth signifies is the therapeutic anamnesis of contents which...should never be forgotten for long." The survival of the trickster into modern times, Jung argues, "is mainly due to the interest which the conscious mind brings to bear on him, the inevitable concomitant being...the gradual civilizing, i.e., assimilation, of a primitive daemonic figure...."[5] In short, by raising the symbol of this primitive personality component to consciousness, the trickster myth serves the cause of psychic integration.

In light of the argument I have been presenting in this book—that popular art serves the same integrative function as myths, fairy tales and "visionary" literature—we should not be surprised to find the trickster among the frequently recurring characters in movies, television shows, comic books, and so forth. And in fact, even a casual glance at the *dramatis personae* of popular culture reveals a profusion of trickster-figures.

Who exactly is the trickster? What are his distinguishing traits? Perhaps the best way to define his features is by looking closely at one of his recent and most representative incarnations. For this purpose I have chosen Robert Crumb's "underground" comic strip character Squirrely the Squirrel, who, though far more obscure than his cartoon-cousins Bugs Bunny, Donald Duck, Woody Woodpecker and so on, is nonetheless more typical in many ways of the archaic trickster deities described by Radin and Jung. Though Crumb is generally regarded by critics as an astute social satirist, a countercultural Feiffer,[6] his work, as we have seen in the case of "Whiteman," is informed by a powerful mythopoeic imagination. In one respect, "Squirrely the Squirrel"[7] is indeed a sharp reflection of American society in the sixties, a commentary on the terrifying escalation of violence which characterized our culture in those years. The story is a kind of comic strip equivalent of a movie like *The Wild Bunch,* as if a "Tom and Jerry" short had been directed by Sam Peckinpah. Crumb's status as an underground artist, freed from the restrictions of the official Comics Code Authority, allows him to take the stock situation of the "funny animal" cartoons—in which cats and mice, foxes and crows, coyotes and roadrunners merrily shoot, stab and toss bombs at each other—and make its latent sadism overt. In so doing, he manages to create not only a pointed critique of contemporary American life but also a character whose demonic nature is very close to that of the primordial trickster gods: "brutal, savage beings" known for their "pointless orgies of destruction."[8]

The story opens on a bright spring day in the sugary, pastoral landscape that is the characteristic setting of the "funny animal" cartoon—a fairy tale world of gently rolling hills and gingerbread cottages nestled in sunny glades. At a glance, Squirrely himself ("the nuttiest li'l guy that ever walked across a piece o' paper") seems indistinguishable from hundreds of other endearing cartoon characters, the happy anthropomorphic inhabitants of the land of Disney and Looney Tunes. Dressed like a schoolboy in short pants and shoes, with little white gloves on his hands (for some reason, an obligatory part of every cartoon animal's costume), Squirrely greets us in the first panel with a wink and a wave as he strolls along the path leading from his tree house. "Think I'll go see what that ol' crud Farnsworth the Fox is up to," he says. "Maybe he'll try to catch me an' eat me up again like he always does!! Yuk, yuk!"

The seeming innocence of this panel is undercut, however, by the grin on Squirrely's face and the peculiar glint in his eyes. Crumb, a brilliant draftsman, is a master at providing his characters with enormously expressive features; and in the case of "Squirrely the Squirrel," he has given his hero a look of malicious glee that is particularly disquieting in a figure we automatically associate with such adorable sorts as Chip 'n' Dale and Mickey Mouse. We expect lovable, childlike mischief from these puckish little characters, but what we see in Squirrely's eyes is active malevolence—a streak of sadism that evokes the reform school more than the playground. The casual vulgarity of his language, too—no character in a Disney cartoon would ever call another an "ol' crud"—suggests that, if Mickey and his pals are like a bunch of rollicking children, Squirrely is a juvenile delinquent in rodent disguise.

Whistling a tune, Squirrely ambles over to "Farny's" place, where he finds his old adversary engaged in an uncharacteristic activity. The fox, dressed in a short-sleeved sport shirt and what appear to be work jeans, is down on one knee, trowel in hand, tending a small vegetable patch. "Hey Farny, you stupid jerk!!

What're you doin'?" says Squirrely, malice burning brightly in his eyes. At this moment, an interesting transformation takes place in the comic. Abruptly, with no transition at all, Crumb changes the locale of the story from the forest to a small and characterless suburb: where trees and lush foliage grew an instant ago, we now see telephone poles and tract houses (fig. 1).

This sudden shift from the sunny Green World of the conventional "funny animal" cartoon to a dreary modern suburb is consistent with Crumb's fascination with middle-class milieus.[9] At the same time, the unsightliness of the setting functions as an objective correlative of the protagonist's repellent personality, his ugliness of character, which the superficial sweetness of his appearance only serves to highlight.

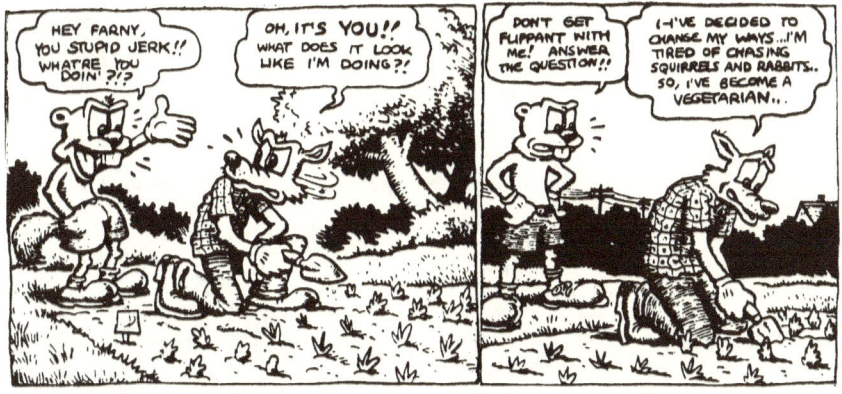

Reprinted with permission from R. Crumb for panels from "Squirrely the Squirrel."

To Squirrely's dismay, Farny announces that he has begun a new life: "I-I've decided to change my ways . . . I'm tired of chasing squirrels and rabbits . . . so I've become a vegetarian." Instead of responding with sense of relief, the squirrel is visibly displeased by the fox's sudden conversion. As Farny, with the pride of a new papa, displays his "organic vegetable garden"—"I'm putting in carrots, turnips . . . radishes over there . . . tomatoes on that end"— Squirrely stands nearby, hand on chin, frowning pensively, clearly not paying the least bit of attention to Farny's inventory but considering how best to handle this unexpected turn of events. Quite casually, he begins to "tromp" on Farny's garden. "Squirrely!! Please don't step on those baby plants!!!" the fox implores. "You'll kill them!!" "Huh??" says Squirrely.

"Wuddjisay?"

As our "li'l" hero, with vicious laughter, continues to stamp more and more violently on the beloved plants, Farny grows increasingly frantic, shouting to the squirrel to stop. Squirrely isn't satisfied, however, until the infuriated fox, eyes turning crazy spirals, grabs his trowel and begins to chase his small tormentor. Face beaming with joy, fully alive now that he has shattered Farny's idyll and lashed him into a murderous frenzy, Squirrely takes off in a flash, crying "Ya can't catch me!! Nyaah!!" As he dashes by Farny's tool shed, Squirrely's gaze falls on a bottle of deadly "insect killer," labelled with skull and crossbones. Farny stops short, his face twisted with fear. "Careful!" he cries, as Squirrely pulls off the cap. "It's very strong! You shouldn't breathe the fumes even!" "Just what th' doctor ordered!!" Squirrely giggles and splashes the contents of the bottle into Farny's face. As Farny, blinded by the chemical, screeches in agony, Squirrely runs off chuckling. "Ta ha ha!! I love to agitate him" (fig. 2).

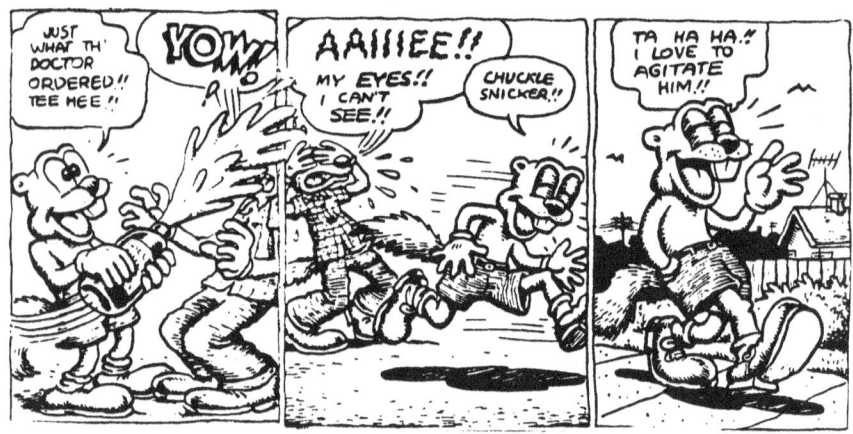

Reprinted with permission from R. Crumb for panels from "Squirrely the Squirrel."

The final section of the story takes place on the following day. Interestingly, Crumb shifts the setting once again, this time to the city. Against a background of dingy stores and tenements, Squirrely, slouching along the streets, seems more than ever the sadistic punk, aimless and looking for trouble. "I'm bored," he complains, but his face suddenly brightens as he sees the blinded Farny—wearing dark glasses now and carrying a cane—come tap-tapping down the sidewalk. The gentle Farny seems to bear no grudges against his assailant. "Squirrely! Is that you. Could you spare me a nickel? I'm broke and hungry." "Sure! Here!" says Squirrely—and, with an exaggerated wink at the audience, he hands the hapless Farny a burning match (fig. 3). Farny, his hand singed, screams in pain, then goes berserk and begins strangling Squirrely—only to be attacked himself by a young female passerby, who pounds the fox with her pocketbook. "You fiend," she cries. "Unhand that poor defenseless little squirrel!" Seeing the commotion, a cop rushes over, beats Farny over the head with his nightstick, and hauls him off to jail, where he won't be able to "pick on helpless little squirrels anymore." The last two panels show Farny languishing in prison while Squirrely reclines on the lap of the young lady who came to his aid. "Does that feel better, sweet baby?" she coos. Squirrely just grins evilly and laughs. "Ain't I a devil? Heh heh!"

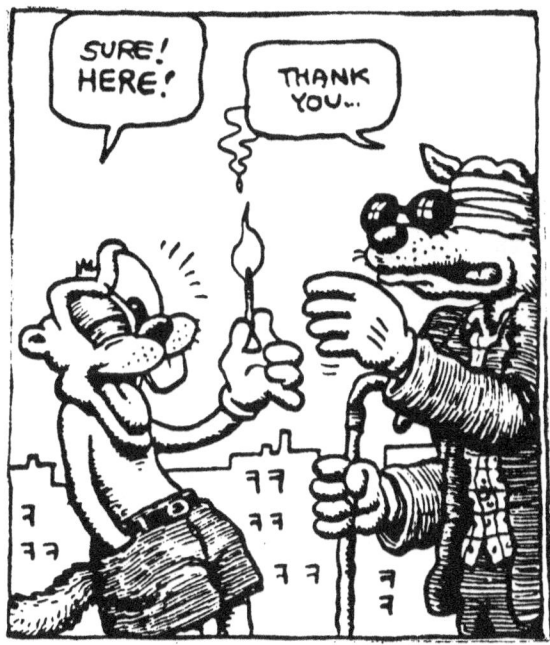

Reprinted with permission from R. Crumb for panels from "Squirrely the Squirrel."

It is possible, of course, to read this comic as one of Crumb's "powerful cultural critique[s]"[10]—a commentary on the terrifying rise of teenage crime, for instance, or a cynical statement about the American system of justice. It seems to me, however, that the story is less compelling as a piece of social criticism than as the portrayal of a figure who, in Jung's words, "haunts the mythology of all ages."[11] In Squirrely the Squirrel we see all the characteristics of the archetypal trickster. As the symbol of a "rudimentary stage of consciousness"[12]—of an early step in man's evolution toward a more highly developed state—the trickster-figure frequently takes the form of an animal or a child. Squirrely, as we have seen, is both: a squirrel anthropomorphically portrayed as a juvenile delinquent. Moreover, like Squirrely, the trickster always gives the appearance of powerlessness, helplessness, either by virtue of his small physical stature (in comparison to the size of his adversary) or, at times, because of his inferior social position, his membership in an oppressed or exploited group.

But the trickster's primary trait is the pleasure he takes in causing trouble. As we see in Squirrely's beaming face—in his unbounded delight when he wrecks Farny's placid existence—the trickster is a being who is happiest when he is creating chaos, disturbing the peace. Farny's new-found contentment is intolerable to Squirrely, for—just as Nature abhors a vacuum—the trickster cannot abide tranquility. He is a compulsive prankster, a lover of anarchy, pandemonium, discord, who, in Jung's words, "does the most atrocious things" for the sheer joy of doing them.[13]

This central feature of the trickster's personality is vividly illustrated in an anecdote Joseph Campbell relates in *Hero With a Thousand Faces*. The tale, from Yorubaland in West Africa, concerns a trickster-divinity named Edshu:

One day, this odd god came walking along a path between two fields. "He beheld in either field a farmer at work and proposed to play the two a turn. He donned a hat that was on the one side red but on the other white...so that when the two friendly farmers had gone home to their village and the one had said to the other, 'Did you see that old fellow go by today in the white hat?' the other replied, 'Why the hat was red.' To which the first retorted 'It was not; it was white.' 'But it was red,' insisted the friend, 'I saw it with my own two eyes.' 'Well, you must be blind,' declared the first. 'You must be drunk,' rejoined the other. And so the argument developed and the two came to blows. When they began to knife each other, they were brought by neighbors before the headman for judgment. Edshu was among the crowd at the trial, and when the headman sat at a loss to know where justice lay, the old trickster revealed himself, made known his prank, and showed the hat.

'The two could not help but quarrel,' he said. 'I wanted it that way. Spreading strife is my greatest joy.' ' "[14]

The casual cruelty displayed by Edshu and Squirrely is characteristic of the trickster. Wadjunkaga, the hero of the Winnebago Indian myths recorded by Radin, is capable of astonishing acts of brutality. In one of the episodes in the cycle, for instance, he persuades a pair of raccoon-women to leave their babies with him, promising to look after the little ones while the females go off to search for some fruit. No sooner are they out of sight, however, than the trickster kills the children, cooks and devours them. But the worst is yet to come, for "when he was finished, he cut off the head of one of the children, put a stick through its neck and placed it at the door [of the lodge] as though the child were peeping and laughing." When the mothers return—in a sour mood because they have been unable to find any fruit—they see the child peeking through the door, apparently laughing at them, and in irritation, one of them slaps the baby on the cheek, knocking the head off the pole on which it has been impaled. "There, much to her horror, she noticed that it was only the child's head. Then both of the women cried out, 'Oh, my children! He has killed them. It must have been trickster!'... They wept very much."[15]

It is easy to see that, though the trickster is usually a humorous character whose antics are meant to make us laugh—a jester, practical joker, or clown—he has a darker aspect which is savage, even satanic. Indeed, the merry prankster of comedy may easily become, in more serious literature, the devil himself. That Satan is, in fact, closely related to the trickster can be seen, according to Jung, "in the mediaeval description of the devil as 'simia dei' (the ape of God)."[16] This relationship is also evident in Elizabethan drama. The first English comedy, Nicholas Udall's *Ralph Roister Doister* (1552) features a mischievous character named Matthew Merygreeke—a figure modelled after the Plautine "tricky servant"—who spends all his time humiliating the pompous hero Ralph by making him the butt of endless practical jokes. True trickster that he is, Matthew admits at one point that he prefers fun to food:

But such sport have I with him as I would not lese,

Though I should be bound to live with bread and cheese.[17]

Transposed to tragedy, however, the same kind of character—the singleminded manipulator and humiliator of other people—becomes monstrous: Matthew Merygreeke turns into Iago. The answer to the perennially perplexing question of Iago's motivation can be found, it seems to me, in the African story of Edshu. Like all trickster-figures, Iago causes havoc because it is part of his nature—because it *is* his nature—to do so. As Edshu explains, "Spreading strife is my greatest joy!" (Or as Squirrely the Squirrel puts it, "I love to agitate him!") This satanic side of the trickster can still be seen in comic book villains like the Green Goblin, a demonic creature dressed in a bizarre Halloween costume and armed with a bagful of lethal tricks (from *Spider-man* comics); the Prankster, one of Superman's old enemies, who commits crimes by means of elaborate practical jokes; and the Joker, the harlequin-faced archfiend of *Batman* comics.

Unlike such primitive figures as Edshu and Wadjunkaga, however, most of the tricksters that appear in modern popular culture are more cuddly than cruel—cute little mischief-makers in the shape of "funny animals" like Heckle and Jeckle, Woody Woodpecker and Sylvester the Cat. As I suggested in the opening chapter, contemporary popular culture reflects the same process of bowdlerization evident in Victorian versions of the original Grimm Brothers' fairy tales. When a daemon emerges into modern, mainstream popular art, it does so only after passing through a series of censoring agencies (the Comics Code Authority, for instance, as well as the creator's own conception of his readers' pristine sensibilities) which inevitably deplete it of some—though by no means all—of its primordial power. It appears, in short, in a watered-down form. The transformation of the trickster from a malicious jokester into a lovable "li'l devil" can be seen in the evolution of the character Bugs Bunny, whose mythological ancestry can be traced back to a pair of primitive rabbit-heroes, the West African trickster "Soamba," and the Winnebago Indian trickster "Hare."

In the black folktales of the American South, these two creatures are synthesized in the figure of Brer Rabbit, whose behavior is, on occasion, shockingly savage. In the story "How

Brer Dog Lost His Beautiful Voice," for instance, Brer Rabbit, jealous of Brer Dog's singing abilities (the latter has won the heart of the lovely "Miss Saphronie" by serenading her each night), tricks the dog into opening wide his mouth, then splits the poor animal's tongue with a razor blade.[18] In the late 1930s, this unruly folk figure—whose antics had been popularized (and somewhat toned down) by Joel Chandler Harris in his collections of "Uncle Remus" stories (published between 1880 and 1918)— reappeared in the form of the wisecracking cartoon character Bugs Bunny, who can still be seen on TV every Saturday morning, making life miserable for his favorite "fall guy," Elmer Fudd.

Though the trickster-figures we have looked at so far have been actual creatures of various kinds—squirrels, rabbits and so forth—certain tricksters take the form of characters whose animality is figurative rather than literal. The heroes of the movie *National Lampoon's Animal House,* for instance—the "animals" of the Delta fraternity at mythical Faber College— have earned their epithet because of their unbridled behavior. The spirit of Delta House is embodied in the person of Bluto Blutarsky (played by John Belushi), an unspeakably gross character who seems barely a step above Cro-Magnon man on the evolutonary ladder: who guzzles beer by the kegful for breakfast, drunkenly urinates on the shoes of nearby strangers, demolishes whole rooms full of furniture at the slightest provocation, moves along the cafeteria line sucking up food like an anteater, and communicates largely in snorts, grunts and yowls.

The movie's plot (such as it is) deals with the ongoing battle between the anarchistic animals of Delta House and the forces of conformity and authoritarianism, as represented by the Deltas' hated rivals, the militaristic brothers of Omega House, and their commander-in-chief, the tyrannical Dean Wormer.[19] Though the film is clearly a low-budget production and often amateurish, it did phenomenally well at the box office. Its great popularity—a surprise even to its creators—testifies, I believe, to the enduring appeal of the trickster archetype. As a cinematic representation of the trickster, Belushi's marginally human Bluto is, in its way, unrivalled, and undoubtedly accounts in large measure for the movie's success. Even the crudeness, the primitivity of the film— its choppy editing, cheap look and narrative incoherencies—

serve to convey the essence of the trickster, as does the puerility of the humor, which consists entirely of very broad slapstick and childish, vulgar jokes. As I have said, the child is another guise the trickster typically assumes, not only because, like the animal, it serves as a natural symbol for a rudimentary stage of consciousness, but also because the trickster, as a form of the collective shadow, is specifically an embodiment of "puerile and inferior" personality traits.[20] Moreover, young children often display the same capacity for destruction as undomesticated animals—a quality acknowledged in the title of a recent handbook for parents, *Baby Taming*.[21]

Though the trickster can sometimes appear as a female child (the comic strip character Little Iodine is a good example), a much more common form of the archetype—and an especially prevalent one in our culture—is the bad boy. According to Leslie Fiedler, the "crude and unruly" but true-hearted young rascal—the figure Fiedler calls the Good Bad Boy—represents "America's vision of itself,"[22] and there is no doubt that this particular incarnation of the trickster holds a special meaning for the American imagination. Though this image continues to exert an enormous appeal, as the success of *Animal House* demonstates, the heyday of the bad boy in our popular art was the late nineteenth-century, when he flourished in such bestselling books as Mark Twain's *The Adventures of Tom Sawyer* and *Adventures of Huckleberry Finn,* Thomas Bailey Aldrich's *The Story of a Bad Boy,* Booth Tarkington's Penrod novels, and—perhaps the quintessential literature of this kind—George W. Peck's "Peck's Bad Boy" collections, the best known of which is the 1883 volume *Peck's Bad Boy and His Pa.*

These stories were originally published as newspaper pieces and, like every ongoing popular series, from TV sitcoms to the novels of Mickey Spillane, they follow an unvarying formula. As a result, reading through an entire collection of them quickly becomes tedious. Individual episodes, however, can still entertain: they are fast-paced, full of energy and often very funny, though the comedy is unquestionably low and unrefined. Even so, it is hard to do good slapstick in prose, and Peck, though a primitive stylist, knows how to elicit a bellylaugh. Moreover, within the fixed format he has established, he displays considerable ingenuity in inventing new ways for young

Hennery, the hero of the tales, to torment his victims. In each of the stories, the Bad Boy pays a visit to the "groceryman" to boast of his most recent bit of "deviltry": invariably, a sadistic prank the youngster has contrived to humiliate his pompous "old man." Meanwhile, even as he describes his latest practical joke, we see him working a new one on the hapless grocer. Since one episode in this series is much the same as the next, a single example will serve to convey the flavor of the whole.

"His Pa is a Darn Coward" is an early episode in the series, appearing as Chapter Six of *Peck's Bad Boy and His Pa*. Like all the tales in this collection, this is a "framework" story set inside the grocery store, where the Bad Boy has come to chat with (and as it turns out, to pull a fast one on) the proprietor. While the grocer is busy "putting up some canned goods for the boy, who said the goods were for the folks to use at a picnic, but which was to be taken out camping by the boy and his chum," Hennery lounges about, "trying a new can opener on a tin biscuit box." Very matter-of-factly, he launches into an account of his latest piece of mischief: "I suppose you think my Pa is a brave man," he begins. "O, I suppose he is," replies the grocer as he bills the goods to the boy's father. "Your Pa is called a major, and you know at the time of the re-union he wore a veteran badge, and talked to the boys about how they suffered during the war." This credulous response only draws a sneer from the boy. "Suffered nothing," he scoffs, "unless they suffered from the peach brandy and leather pies Pa sold them." Pa, it turns out, was a "suttler" during the war—a camp follower peddling supplies to the soldiers—"and he is," the boy asserts with the utter disrespect that distinguishes his relationship with his father, "a coward." Hennery, meanwhile, has been surreptitiously slipping "sweet crackers" inside his pants' pocket and under his shirt; but, though the merchant notices this petty thievery, he says nothing, intimidated as always by the coolness of the boy, whom he regards as a "hard citizen." Obviously the grocer believes that it is better to sacrifice a few biscuits to the Bad Boy than to risk provoking him. And indeed, the anecdote Hennery proceeds to relate justifies the grocer's wariness of this juvenile, who derives so much enjoyment from degrading his elders.

The Bad Boy informs the store owner that ever since a recent robbery at a neighbor's house, his father has been bragging about what he would do if burglars ever broke into *his* house. "He said he would jump out of bed and knock one senseless with his fist, and throw the other over the banister." Pa, in short, is a nineteenth century American avatar of the *miles gloriosus*. Smug and bombastic, this kind of character is a perfect foil for, and favorite victim of, the trickster. (Just as Matthew Merygreeke in Nicholas Udall's *Ralph Roister Doister* is based on the "tricky slave" of Roman New Comedy, so the title character is explicitly modelled on the Plautine braggart soldier.)

The traits displayed by Pa—his bluster, conceit and sanctimoniousness—are a red flag to the irreverent Hennery, who, in typical trickster fashion, perceives his father as a windbag just begging to be impaled. To that end, he convinces a "chum" to assist him in a little scheme. Dressed like burglars with masks over their faces and caps pulled low over their eyes, the two sneak into the bedroom of the Bad Boy's parents one night. Hennery, carrying a "meerschaum pipe case" with a piece of ice tied to the end, walks over to the bed, places "the cold muzzle of the ice revolver" against his sleeping pa's temple, and, when his father awakens, tells him that "if he moved a muscle or said a word I would splatter the wall and the counterpane with his brains." Pa—apparently so blinded by fright that he fails to notice the unusually small size of the criminals—instantly begins to quake, sweat, pray and grovel. He points out the location of all the cash and valuables in the house and abjectly pleads with the Bad Boy: "Please, Mr. Burglar, take all I have got, but spare a poor old man's life who never did any harm!" Though a different kind of son might, at this point, be moved to compassion by the pathetic sight of a father reduced to such a state of cringing fear, Hennery has one last humiliation in store for his Pa. Ordering him to turn over "on his stomach and pull the clothes over his head, and stick his feet over the foot board," the Bad Boy takes a "shawl strap" and begins tying his father's legs together—when his Ma awakens and asks what is going on. Hennery informs her that he is a "burglar, robbing the house," but Ma, who doesn't scare quite as easily as her husband, tells the masked intruder to "get out of here or I'll take you across my knees," then jumps out of bed and starts chasing the boy and his chum. They flee to the Bad Boy's room, but Ma follows them there and, grabbing up Pa's "jointed fishing pole," gives them both a hearty "mauling." "I didn't know Ma had so much sand," says the boy, half ruefully, half admiringly. "She is as brave as a lion, but Pa is a regular squaw." Having decided that it is best to make himself scarce for a while, until the incident has blown over, the Bad Boy is on his way to Pewaukee "to camp out" with his chum. And so he departs, taking the "canned ham and lobster" which he has led the grocer to believe are for his parents, and tucking a few last crackers inside his flannel shirt.[23]

The image of the typical American family portrayed in this tale—of the foolish, ineffectual father and the stern, forceful wife—is deeply embedded in the American psyche. In our culture, it is as old as the legend of Hannah Duston and Irving's "Rip Van Winkle" and as recent as the latest television sitcom featuring a fumbling husband—à la Dagwood Bumstead—and his strong and competent wife. The meaning of this archetypal image of American man-and-womanhood, however, is outside the scope of this study.[24] And the Oedipal fantasy which finds expression in this anecdote—indeed in all of the Peck's Bad Boy stories—is so clear that it requires no explication. What *is* worth examining in regard to these tales is the reason for their popular success (which was so great that their creator was twice elected governor of Wisconsin). How do we account for the enormous appeal of a character as amoral as the Bad Boy, a child who lies, cheats, steals and exhibits undisguised contempt for the Fifth Commandment?

Part of the answer, I believe, is that Hennery is an epitome of Gilded Age virtues, an ideal hero for that era, displaying all the qualities—"gumption," cunning, cool-headedness and a flair for finagling—which guarantee a young man a bright financial future. As Peck himself says near the very start of his book, "Of course all boys are not full of tricks, but the best of them are. That is, those who are readiest to play innocent jokes, and who are continually looking for chances to make Rome howl, are the most apt to turn out to be first-class business men."[25]

But the primary reason for the great popularity of these skits, I believe, is that Hennery is such a perfect representation of the archetypal trickster. In Peck's Bad Boy we see what Jung would call the "autochthonous emergence" of an archetypal image from the depths of the collective unconscious; and in the enormous appeal which these stories exerted on a very wide audience, we see evidence of the "numinous" power produced by such symbols.

Like all mythological figures, that is to say, Hennery represents the conjunction of archetype and history, the "universal" incarnating itself in the "local."

On the one hand, as I have already indicated, this character is a product of his times, a reflection of the cultural values operating in a specific place at a particular historical moment. But beneath the cultural trappings we find the timeless features of a mythological figure. Peck's Bad Boy, in short, is a primordial image clothed in the garb—the knickers and blue flannel shirt— of a typical turn-of-the-century all-American boy. All the traits which distinguish Hennery's behavior are, in fact, archetypal characteristics. His love of disguise, for instance, is an attribute he shares with tricksters throughout the world, from the Norse god Loki, known as the "shape-shifter," to the Winebago hero Wadjunkaga, who at one point in the cycle transforms himself into a woman, up to such a recent incarnation as Bluto Blutarsky of *Animal House,* whom we last see dressed in the costume of a cutlass-wielding pirate. Even the stock ending of these stories— virtually all of which conclude with the Bad Boy's being caught and beaten by one or the other of his parents—is typical of trickster myths, which often show the hero getting punished for his pranks or falling victim to one of them himself (a motif known as "the trickster tricked").

In one of the later Peck's Bad Boy skits, Pa—after suffering countless physical and psychological tortures at the hands of his son—finally gets revenge when he convinces Hennery (who is eager to grow whiskers) that the best way for him to make his moustache grow quickly is to rub tar on his upper lip each night and scrub it off each morning with a scouring-brick. Wadjunkaga, the Winnebago trickster, is often outsmarted by other, more cunning creatures, such as the mink and the chipmunk, and is even, at times, undone by his own unpredictable body. One well-known myth of Wadjunkaga tells of the day his two arms began battling each other over a slain buffalo which the trickster had been skinning—a fight which ended only after the knife-wielding right hand had severely wounded the left. And cartoon schemers like Wile E. Coyote of the "Roadrunner" shorts are always being snared by the elaborate booby-traps they have set up for others.

But the quality of the trickster which perhaps more than any other explains why Americans take such delight in him is his contempt for social pretension, for people who put on airs. Seeing pomposity deflated has always been one of the pleasures afforded by trickster stories: it is a theme with universal appeal. But it is also one to which American audiences have always responded with particular satisfaction, partly, I think, because it relieves a deep-seated sense of social inferiority before polished manners and Old World sophistication. This trait has made the trickster one of the favorite character-types in American culture, not only in the form of the child, but also in that of the con man (a figure who, in various guises, has always enjoyed great popularity in this country, from the slick Yankee peddler of eighteenth-century folklore through Mark Twain's marvelous "hum-bugs," the Duke and Dauphin, and up to such recent mass media examples as television's Sergeant Bilko and Hogan's Heroes).

The treatment which the high and the mighty receive at the hands of the trickster, in fact, has at all times made him a favorite folk hero of people who are looked upon as, or who feel themselves to be, lowly or inferior. Clearly one of the psychological functions of the trickster myth is that it compensates for feelings of impotence in the face of large, oppressive power. It is for this reason that the trickster appears so often in fairy tales. Stories of seemingly insignificant beings—small boys or dwarfs—who use their wits to defeat giants and ogres serve to reinforce the child's ego. It is for this reason, too, that the trickster, in the form of such folk heroes as Brer Rabbit and Stackolee, was so popular among the American slaves. The trickster-figure can even appear in an individual's fantasies (as opposed to the collective ones of a powerless, despised, or downtrodden group) to compensate for personal feelings of inferiority, as the example of Edgar Allan Poe's "Hop-Frog" seems to suggest.

The "large, corpulent, oily" king who meets such a gruesome end at the hands of Poe's misshapen hero is a prototypical foe of the trickster-figure, whose adversaries are always embodiments of established power, representatives of a rigid social order in relation to which the trickster functions as the agent of an irrepressible energy. Thus the usual setting for trickster stories is some strict, hierarchical system or institution—the military, the university, "high society"—whose exemplars become the inevitable targets of the anarchistic hero. As we have seen, the fraternity brothers of *Animal House* are committed to the

complete destruction of their college's disciplinarian dean. The
Marx Brothers—the preeminent trickster-figures of the screen—
are never happier than when they are demolishing the dignity of
a supercilious aristocrat, making a haughty "society dame" look
stupid, or wreaking havoc in an opera house. Sergeant Bilko's
perennial patsy is the powerful army "brass," embodied in the
person of his straight-laced superior officer, Colonel J.T. Hall,
while Hogan's Heroes are continually making fools of the
bombastic Nazi, Commandant Klink, and his strutting sidekick,
Sergeant Schulz.

It is in the trickster's relation to repressive authority that we
see the positive aspect of this unpredictable mythological figure.
As a manifestation of the collective shadow, the trickster
symbolizes primitive, instinctual forces with great potential for
destruction. In our personal lives, for instance, the trickster
makes itself felt as that seemingly diabolical element in the
human psyche which bridles at serenity, which cannot tolerate
too prolonged a period of happiness and peace. Poe called this
element "the Imp of the Perverse," describing it as a primitive
impulse which causes us to do the wrong thing precisely "because
we feel that we should *not.*"[26] This is the side of the trickster
symbolized by such malicious troublemakers as Edshu and
Squirrely the Squirrel. But the paradoxical fact about the
trickster is that he is a creator as well as a destroyer. "A fool, and a
cruel, lecherous cheat, an epitome of the principle of disorder, he is
nevertheless the culture bringer also," writes Joseph Campbell.[27]

In the myths of certain American Indian tribes, for example,
it is the trickster-figure (in the form of Coyote, Raven or Hare,
depending on the particular tribe) who steals fire from the Fire
People and passes it along to mankind. Psychologically
speaking, the trickster archetype in its more positive form stands
for that life-affirming part of ourselves which retains a healthy
disrespect for the authoritanian, the regimented, the
pretentious—that part which, despite the best efforts of society to
tame it, remains filled with a kind of animal vitality and childlike
spontaneity. It is because the trickster-figure embodies these
qualities that the works in which he appears—movies, comic
books, cartoons, etc.—are so often distinguished by a wild,
unbounded energy which makes them appealing even when (like
Animal House) they are poorly made. Of course, these are not

qualities which the disciplinarian holds very dear; but insofar as they impel us to struggle against those forces that would stifle or subdue us (extreme social conformity, for example) they are indispensable. As Joseph Campbell puts it, "from the point of view of the masters of decorum," the trickster represents "the chaos principle...the force careless of taboos and shattering bounds. But from the point of view of the deeper realms of being from which the energies of life ultimately derive, this principle is not to be despised."[28] Like primitive myths and fairy tales, popular art works to widen the consciousness of its audience by bringing this vital personality component to the fore.

2

Throughout this study I have been suggesting that there is an intimate connection between contemporary popular culture and the fairy tale. Indeed, it seems to me that—though most critics continue to talk about movies and the like in language drawn from traditional literary scholarship—popular art has closer affinities with fairy tales than with "high" or "serious" literature. Other writers have noted this relationship. In *Seduction of the Innocent,* Frederic Wertham quotes the comments of several unnamed "comic book experts," one of whom observes that "comic books [are] in a way parallel to some of the fairy tales such as *Beauty and the Beast, Hansel and Gretel* and *The Pied Piper of Hamlin...,*" while another points out that "psychologically the comics are the modern fairy tales."[29] Wertham, the Carrie Nation of comicdom, has no use for such apologists, and flatly denies their assertions: "comic books have nothing in common with [fairy tales]. Fairy tales have a magic of their own which is completely absent from comic books....Comic books are not dreamlike and not symbolic."[30] To be fair to Wertham, whose hysterical tone and heavy-handed Freudianism are easy enough to poke fun at, the comics he focused his attack on—the crime magazines so popular during the nineteen forties and fifties—were indeed pretty pathological, owing more to de Sade than to Jacob and Wilhelm Grimm. But what Wertham, caught up in his singleminded crusade, never saw was the number of comics which do portray the magical, the marvelous, the mythical.

One of the characteristics of popular culture which makes

clear its connection to myth and fairy tale is its treatment of animals. It is difficult, if not impossible, to think of a work of serious literature in which an animal figures as an important character (even Moby Dick does not appear until the last few chapters of Melville's novel; and in any case, the white whale is less a character than an awesome, inscrutable *force*). But in comic books, movies and television shows—as in fairy tales—animals play central roles all the time. One of these roles, as we have seen, is that of the trickster. Another equally important and prevalent one is that of the hero's servant and companion, a figure known in folklore as the helpful animal.

The helpful animal represents the positive aspect of the collective shadow; it is the symbol of instinct working in harmony with ego, of man's animal nature as a guiding, supportive and revitalizing force. As Bruno Bettelheim makes abundantly clear in *The Uses of Enchantment*, a major theme in fairy tales is the necessity of achieving psychic integration though the assimilation of our "instinctual drives"—a theme symbolized by the common motif in which a hero is assisted in a difficult task by friendly creatures of various kinds.

In the Grimm Brothers' story "The Queen Bee," for example, the young hero, Simpleton, must perform three deeds to deliver a castle from enchantment. The first is to find a thousand pearls which are scattered in a forest, beneath the mossy floor. If he has not recovered every single pearl by sunset, he will be turned to stone. Baffled by the impossibility of this task, he sits down to weep, when a colony of ants he has previously saved from destruction suddenly appears and fetches the jewels. In his second and third tasks he is likewise assisted by "grateful animals" whose lives he has saved: some ducks, who retrieve a sunken key from the bottom of the lake, and the Queen of the bees, who helps him identify a sleeping princess.

Similarly, the hero of the fairy tale "The Three Feathers" (whose name is also Simpleton) finds himself faced with three hopeless challenges: to bring his father, the king, the most beautiful carpet, ring and woman in the world, and thereby inherit the kingdom. Like his namesake in "The Queen Bee," young Simpleton sits down sadly and utterly at a loss, only to discover a trap-door leading down to the abode of a "great fat toad," who magically supplies him with the treasures he seeks. In fairy tales, explains Bettelheim, "both dangerous and helpful animals stand for our animal nature, our instinctual drives. The dangerous ones symbolize the untamed id, not yet subjected to ego and superego control, in all its dangerous energy. The helpful animals represent our natural energy—again the id—but now made to serve the best interests of the total personality." Thus, the message communicated to the unconscious of young readers by fairy tales like "The Queen Bee" and "The Three Feathers" is that "only when animal nature has been befriended, recognized as important, and brought into accord with ego and superego does it lend its power to the total personality. After we have thus achieved an integrated personality, we can accomplish what seem like miracles."[31]

The myths and legends of the world similarly teach the importance of befriending the impersonal shadow, of respecting and paying heed to that animal part of the human personality which society encourages us to regard as worthless and inferior. In his book *The King and the Corpse*, the famous German Indologist, Heinrich Zimmer, relates the "ancient pagan myth" of the Irish hero Conn-eda, who receives guidance and advice on a perilous quest from his "little shaggy horse"—a magical beast which, though unimpressive in appearance, possesses superior wisdom, as well as the power of speech. Commenting on the meaning of the hero's relationship with his horse, Zimmer explains that,

in the picture language of folklore and myth, the symbolic figure of mount and rider represents the centauric character of man, fatefully compounded of animal instinct and human virtue. The horse is the "lower," purely instinctive and intuitive aspect of the human being, the mounted knight the "higher" portion: conscious valor, the moral sense, will power, and reason. Normally, the rider is regarded as the guiding, goal-determining, discriminating member of the fellowship and the steed as merely the servile, though not undignified, vehicle. Here, however, in this pagan Irish myth, it is the knight who submits, humbly, faithfully, letting his reins lie loose on the animal's neck. Conn-eda, this hero of heroes, in his trial-beset passage through the unpredictable realm of nature's chaotic forces...follows without qualm the lead of his "lower" wisdom, the inferior and despised aspect of his centauric nature, the unreasonable, instinctive impulses of his composite being.[22]

Indeed, it is precisely his trust in this "despised aspect of his...nature," his readiness to follow the promptings of instinct, which marks Prince Conn-eda as a genuine hero.

That popular art offers the same psychological truth as fairy tales like "The Queen Bee" and "The Three Feathers" and myths like that of Conn-eda can be seen in the movie version of Jules Verne's *Journey to the Center of the Earth*. This film is a very interesting work—a slick piece of mass entertainment which quite unselfconsciously embodies a host of mythic motifs. Though I intend to discuss this movie in more detail later on, I mention it here because among the many archetypal images it contains is a perfect representation of the helpful animal.

Near the start of the film, at the very outset of the fantastic journey it portrays, Professor Lindenbrook, the leader of the expedition, stands on a ledge inside a volcanic crater, completely at a loss. He cannot locate the concealed opening in the mountainside which will give him access to the earth's interior. Suddenly, Gertrude, the pet duck of one of the explorers and the expedition's mascot, wanders away from the rest of the company and waddles into a small opening in the rock. Needless to say, Gertrude has found the hidden entrance, and Lindenbrook joyfully follows her. The message of this episode is the very one conveyed by the legend of Conn-eda: the helpful animal can be a wonderful ally, but only of those who are willing to pay attention to it. And conversely, one of the traits of the true hero is precisely his willingness to accept the animal's guidance and advice. Lindenbrook, the world-famous scientist, succeeds not only because he is a brilliant thinker but also because he respects and heeds the "wisdom" of a lowly creature like Gertrude the Duck. He succeeds, in short, because he combines both intellect and instinct.

The ideal hero of popular art—as of myth and fairy tale—is, I have pointed out, the complete man, the integrated personality. He is neither spineless "egghead" nor mindless brute but a healthy combination of intelligence, virtue and animal spirits. In opposition to the conventional wisdom of society, which tends to look down on the earthy, physical, instinctual side of human nature and tells us that we should struggle to deny or "rise above" it, the hero recognizes the value of the animal qualities he contains. He understands not only that instinct is sometimes a more reliable guide than pure reason but also that it can be a source of great strength. Far from despising the animal element in himself, he respects it, "befriends" it—surrenders himself to its guidance in humility and trust. And in turn, like the grateful animals of the Grimm Brothers' stories, it repays him with its energies and powers.

In the world of popular culture, then, the hero and his animal associate always form a single unit, one which stands for the fusion of the "higher human qualities of intellect, reason, will power and good will" with the "lower" animal level of our nature.[33] The hero's relationship with the helpful animal is the visible sign of his psychic wholeness—a symbol very similar in meaning to the motif we examined in the previous chapter: the white hero's friendship with an Indian or black. Indeed, the two symbols are often interchangeable, so that we frequently find animals replacing humans in the role of the faithful companion. In *Star Wars,* for example, the trusty sidekick of the swashbuckling space-cowboy Han Solo is a giant, monkey-like creature called a Wookie, the science fiction equivalent of the Lone Ranger's Tonto.

In classic American literature, where "The Myth of the Good Companions in the Wilderness" (as Fiedler calls it) finds its most powerful expression, heroes who lack helpmates from primitive cultures will sometimes be accompanied by loyal animals instead. Perhaps the earliest mythic hero in our fiction, Rip Van Winkle, escapes from his termagent wife in the company of his devoted hound, Wolf; while Natty Bumppo, after the death of his bosom friend Chincachgook, becomes deeply attached to a dog named Hector.

Though dogs commonly play the role of helpful animals in popular culture—Lassie, Rin Tin Tin, Rex the Wonder Dog, Old Yeller, Old Blue and Toto are several well-known examples—the archetype may in fact be embodied by a member of virtually any species. Miraculous creatures of every variety abound in the folktales of all nations, as well as in world mythology and the popular arts. At times, of course, the kind of helpful animal found in a work will depend on the story's locale, so that in jungle adventures, like the Tarzan and Bomba series, the helpful animals are elephants, champanzees and pumas, whereas in an undersea fantasy like *Aquaman* comics, the non-human helpers are the "denizens of the deep": porpoises, stingrays and the like. But of all helpful animals, as the folklorist Stith Thompson points out, "none has been so popular with taletellers as the horse."[34]

Mythology and folklore provide countless examples of magical horses—creatures that can fly, speak and gallop up the sides of glass mountains. In our own time, when popular culture (as I have been arguing) has assumed the function once performed by fairy tales and myths, such marvelous beasts can be seen all the time in movies, comic books, television shows and pulp fiction. Though these creatures sometimes appear in contemporary settings (like the suburban world of *Mr. Ed*) and sometimes in ahistorical ones (such as Middle Earth, the mythical realm of the Tolkien trilogy and home of the incomparable steed Shadowfax), it is the Western frontier, naturally enough, that provides the ideal locale for tales of wonder-horses. Indeed it could be argued that it is the presence of the age-old mythic figure of the Magic Horse which accounts at least in part for the world-wide popularity of American cowboy books and movies.

While Tom Mix, Gene Autry, Roy Rogers and other Hollywood heroes of the nineteen twenties and thirties rode mounts that could perform incredible feats—outrun locomotives, untie knots with their teeth and understand perfectly every word spoken by their masters—the Magic Horse actually appears much earlier as a convention of the Western. The February 1867 issue of *Harper's New Monthly Magazine,* for instance, contains an "Interview with Wild Bill Hickok" which—though presented as purely factual (and apparently accepted as such by contemporary readers), is clearly the work of a mythopoeic imagination. Its author, George Ward Nichols, is lounging in the lobby of the Springfield (Missouri) Hotel when he sees "Wild Bill riding up the street at a swift gallop":

Arrived opposite to the hotel, he swung his right arm around with a circular motion. Black Nell instantly stopped and dropped to the ground as if a cannon-ball had knocked the life out of her. Bill left her there, stretched upon the ground, and joined the group of observers on the porch.

"Black Nell hasn't forgotten her old tricks," said one of them.

"No," answered the scout. "God bless her! she is wiser and truer than most men I know of. That mare will do anything for me. Won't you, Nelly?"

The mare winked affirmatively the only eye we could see.

        *   *   *

"Black Nell has carried me along through many a tight place," said the scout,... "That trick of dropping quick which you saw has saved my life time and

again. When I have been out scouting on the prarer or in the woods, I have come
across parties of rebels, and have dropped out of sight in the tall grass before they
saw us.... The mare will come at my whistle and foller me about just like a dog.
She won't mind any one else, nor allow them to mount her...."

In Black Nell's behavior—and in Wild Bill's relationship
with her—we see all the characteristics of the helpful animal
archetype. Since hero and beast represent two, interconnected
aspects of a single personality, a peculiar intimacy exists between
them. They are, in fact, inseparable: so much so that it is
generally impossible to think of the name of one of the early
cowboy stars without immediately associating him with a horse:
Tom Mix and Tony, Gene Autry and Champion, Roy Rogers and
Trigger, etc. As Black Nell's refusal to allow anyone but Bill to
ride her suggests, the animal *belongs* to the human being: she is a
part of him. This motif is common among folktales featuring
Magic Horses.[36] When dogs play the part of the helpful animal,
we often find an analogous theme, in which the dog will obey
nobody but its master—respond to his whistle alone, come at no
one else's command.

Perfect communication exists between the hero and his
animal helper: when beasts can talk, as in fairy tales, the two can,
of course, converse. But even in the case of a presumably
"realistic" creature like Black Nell we see a horse that knows
English, even if she can't speak it. Moreover, her immediate
response to Bill's unspoken signals is clear indication of their
absolute communion. So close are the hero and the helpful
animal, in fact, that their personalities are interfused: the animal
often seems uncannily human—Black Nell "winks
affirmatively" in answer to Bill's question, Rex the Wonder Dog
chuckles along with his young master at a joke (fig. 4)—while the
human exhibits a kind of animal vitality and vigor.

But the most important of the helpful animal's traits is—as
its name suggests—its ability to rescue the hero from desperate
situations: a talent associated with another significant quality,
its superior intelligence (Black Nell is "wiser...than most men,"
says Bill). What exactly is the meaning of this motif of the animal
which shows great sagacity and acts as the hero's savior? Simply
put, its meaning is that reason alone is sometimes not enough,
that logic has its limitations, that—while there is the wisdom of

the rational mind—there is also the wisdom of instinct and intuition. What stories featuring helpful animals teach us, in short, is that, when we are faced with problems or dilemmas we cannot think our way out of, there is another, instinctive order of knowledge available to us, and we must learn to listen to its guidance. This is the unconscious message communicated by many myths and fairy tales, as well as by "Grade B" Westerns, Tarzan movies, and the adventures of Lassie and Rin Tin Tin. Thus, like the legend of Pegasus and the story of "The Queen Bee," popular art conveys a symbolic meaning which can help us enlarge our personalities, put us in touch with the latent powers of the psyche, achieve the wholeness embodied by the archetypal image of the boy and his dog, the cowboy and his wonder-horse, the jungle lord and the king of the beasts.

Chapter Four
Syzygy:
The Integration of the Anima
1

If the encounter with the shadow is the "apprentice-piece" of the individual's
development, then that with the anima is the "masterpiece."
Jung, "Archetypes of the Collective Unconscious"

IN THE PROCESS of individuation or self-realization, the
confrontation with and acceptance of the shadow represents only
an initial phase, a first step. The second, and in many ways far
more difficult one, involves coming to terms with what Jung calls
the "contrasexual" component in the psyche: the *anima* in men
and the *animus* in women. Jung defines the anima archetype as
an autonomous complex—a kind of splinter personality—within
every man's psyche, comprising all his latent and repressed
feminine character traits. This complex manifests itself in
dreams, myths, folklore and art as a magical fantasy woman—
sometimes benevolent, often dangerous, but always intensely
fascinating. The animus archetype represents the corresponding
contrasexual factor in women.

In his writings, however, Jung devotes far more attention to
the anima than to the animus, primarily because, being male, he
had direct knowledge of the former, and apparently felt capable of
writing with much more authority about it. In general Jung's
psychological theories were derived from his intense experience
of his own inner world and the different psychic entitites, the
archetypal figures, that inhabited it. "Nobody can really
understand these things," he writes of the anima and animus
archetypes, "unless he has experienced them himself."[1] I, too, am
going to focus on the anima in the following discussion, partly for
the same subjective reason Jung does: namely, because, as a
male, I feel more qualified to talk about the psychological make-
up of men than of women. But there is another, more objective and
finally more important reason for my exclusive concern with the

87

anima, with the archetypal feminine.

As I explained in an earlier chapter, analytical psychology holds that myths, fairy tales and visionary art works, as well as dreams, "are compensatory to the conscious attitude." According to Jung, the psyche is self-regulating, and if consciousness—our consciously held attitudes and beliefs, as well as our behavior, insofar as it grows out of those beliefs—if consciousness is one-sided or imbalanced or deviates too much from normality and health, the unconscious will strive to correct the imbalance by communicating a symbol to the conscious mind: the symbol of whatever is being overlooked or neglected or ignored. And since the major imbalance in the conscious attitude of Western culture is its masculine bias, its one-sided patriarchal orientation, we should not be surprised to find the same psychological imperative expressed again and again in our symbolic works of art, including our popular art: namely, the necessity for assimilating the anima.

The spiritual health not only of individual men but of male-dominated Western society in general requires that masculine ego-consciousness—the principle Jung describes as *Logos*—be joined with the inner realm of the feminine: the *Eros* principle. The condition of psychic wholeness and harmony which results from this conjunction is symbolized in various ways: Yin and Yang, the androgyne, and the syzygy—the archetype of the divine pair, as exemplified by the alchemical couple of Solar King and Lunar Queen (fig. 1)—are among the many mythological representations of the union of Logos and Eros. Thus, my concentration on the archetypal feminine reflects the prominence of this primordial image in our mythological art, which shows us repeatedly—indeed, almost obsessively—the benefits which follow from the integration of the anima, as well as the psychological damage the anima can cause when she is habitually suppressed, belittled or disregarded.

The process of coming to know one's anima is clearly depicted in Hawthorne's story "The Vision of the Fountain." In terms of its artistry, this is clearly one of Hawthorne's lesser works, though even so, it cannot be classified as a piece of popular culture. Nevertheless, I mention it here because, though it is generally regarded as nothing more than a charming sketch of little substance, it is really quite remarkable for the depth of its

CONIVNCTIO SIVE
Coitus.

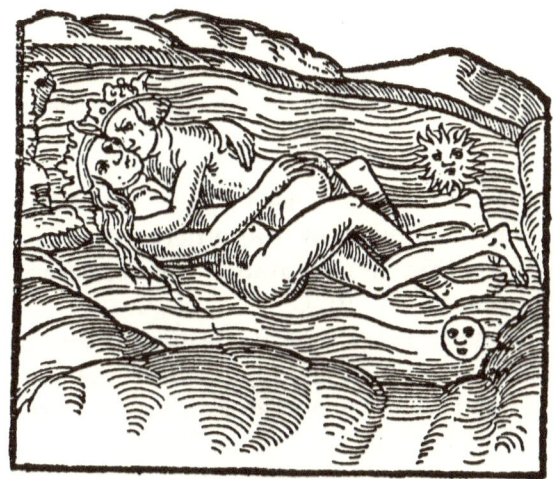

☽ Luna durch meyn vmbgeben/vnd fuffe mynne/
Wirſtu ſchön/ ſtarck/vnd gewaltig als ich byn·

☉ Sol/ du biſt vber alle liecht zu erkennen/
So bedarſſtu doch mein als der han der hennen.

ARISLEVS IN VISIONE.

Coniunge ergo filium tuum Gabricum dile∫
ctiorem tibi in omnibus filijs tuis cum ſua ſorore
Beya

Reprinted with permission from Princeton University Press for the woodcut from *Rosarium Philosophorum, Secunda Pars Alchemiae de Lapide Philosophico* (Frankfurt, 1550). Collection of Dr. C.A. Meier.

psychological insight, and stands as a striking portrayal of the encounter between a man and his anima, or "soul-image," as Jung also calls this archetype.

Rambling through the woods one bright September morning, the young narrator of the tale comes upon a "crystal spring" and stops to gaze at its surface:

Reclining on a border of grass...I bent forward, and a pair of eyes met mine within the watery mirror. They were the reflection of my own. I looked again, and lo! another face, deeper in the fountain than my own image, more distinct in all the features, yet faint as thought. The vision had the aspect of a young girl, with locks of paly gold. A mirthful expression laughed in the eyes and dimpled over the whole shadowy countenance, till it seemed just what a fountain would be, if, while dancing merrily in the sunshine, it should assume the shape of a woman. Through the dim rosiness of the cheeks I could see the brown leaves, the slimy twigs, the acorns, and the sparkling sand. The solitary sunbeam was diffused among the golden hair, which melted into its faint brightness, and became a glory round that head so beautiful.[2]

A moment later the vision fades, and the narrator is left musing about "the rare attributes of that ethereal being." "Was she a water nymph within the fountain," he wonders, "or fairy, or woodland goddess...?" (107).

Like the descent into the cave, the journey through the woods is a universal, mythological symbol of the entry into the unconscious, and what the narrator discovers on this particular psychological voyage is his anima. When Jung describes the meeting with the anima in his essay "Archetypes of the Collective Unconscious," in fact, he refers to the very fantasy that we find in Hawthorne's tale:

Whoever looks into the water sees his own image, but behind it living creatures soon loom up; fishes, presumably, harmless dwellers of the deep—harmless if only the lake were not haunted. They are water-beings of a peculiar sort. Sometimes a nixie gets into the fisherman's net, a female, half-human fish. Nixies are entrancing creatures....

The nixie is an even more instinctive version of a magical feminine being whom I call the *anima*. She can also be a siren, *melusina* (mermaid), wood-nymph, Grace, or Erkling's daughter....[3]

The anima may also appear as a lamia, succubus or Circe: "the lovely siren and the dreadful witch are inseparable," says Edward C. Whitmont. "Fear and attraction...always go together in the confrontation with the world of the absolutely other, the other sex. It is fear of the threateningly unknown and simultaneously a magnetic attraction to this same unknown. By her very nature the anima exerts this arousing and numbing fascination."[4] Contemplating the "dewy goddess," the narrator does, in fact, "shiver pleasantly yet fearfully" (106). But his confrontation with her turns out to be far from harmful, for it leads him to a heightened self-awareness.

According to Jungian theory, when a man is unconscious of the contrasexual part of his personality, he projects it outward with unfortunate results: "a man, in his love choice, is strongly tempted to win the woman who best corresponds to his unconscious femininity—a woman, in short, who can unhesitatingly receive the projection of his soul. Although such a choice is often regarded and felt as altogether ideal, it may turn out that the man has manifestly married his own worst weakness."[5] In order for individuation to proceed, a man must raise his contrasexual side to consciousness—recognize the anima as something within himself, an intrapsychic factor. When this realization occurs, the anima is no longer projected outside onto actual women, but comes to be experienced as a connecting link, a bridge, to the inner realm of emotion, intuition and creativity. The anima thus begins to play the role of the psychopomp, the spiritual guide, "the mediating function between the ego and the inner world."[6]

This realization is precisely what the hero of Hawthorne's tale achieves: he perceives that the bewitching figure is "the daughter of [his] fancy" (107)—something within his own mind. Thereafter, he finds himself drawn "into an inner world, where my thoughts lived and breathed, and the Vision in the midst of them" (108). And when, at the end of the story, he is enchanted by "Rachel...the daughter of the village squire," he recognizes the source of the attraction, understands that he has projected his "Vision" onto the living girl: "If I transformed her to an angel, it is what any youthful lover does for his mistress. Therein consists the essence of my story" (109). The essence of the story, then, is the realization of the anima: the narrator has encountered his soul-image and learned that every man carries a "woman within."

Ed Gentry, the hero of *Deliverance,* comes to a similar realization in the course of the psychological journey that is symbolically depicted in Dickey's novel. We have already discussed this book in terms of the protagonist's discovery of his shadow side. But, as I have said, the acceptance of the shadow is only the first step toward complete self-realization, and there is some evidence in the story that, by the time his adventures are over, Gentry has already embarked on the next phase of the individuation process, the integration of the anima.

Since the anima is, as Marie-Louise von Franz puts it, "a personification of all feminine psychological tendencies in a man's unconscious, such as vague feelings and moods, prophetic hunches, receptiveness to the irrational...and—last but not least—his relation to the unconscious," the strong, though often dimly defined, urge for change and renewal which so many men experience during their middle years is frequently embodied in a bewitching young woman, who rouses them from the deadening routines of their lives. In psychological terms, as von Franz explains in the following passage, what occurs in these cases is the phenomenon known as "anima-projection":

It is the presence of the anima that causes a man to fall suddenly in love when he sees a woman for the first time and knows at once that this is "she."...The projection of the anima in such a sudden and passionate form as a love affair can greatly disturb a man's marriage and can lead to the so-called "human triangle" with its accompanying difficulties. A bearable solution to such a drama can be found only if the anima is recognized as an inner power. The secret aim of the unconscious in bringing about such an entanglement is to force a man to develop and to bring his *own* being to maturity by integrating more of his unconscious personality and bringing it into his real life.[7]

The real solution to the dissatisfaction the individual has been feeling, in short, is not involvement with another woman; true rebirth can come only through establishing a new relationship with the "woman within," with the inner realm of the archetypal feminine.

According to analytical psychology, then, the impulse to "penetrate into the unknown territory of the deep unconscious" is "transmitted to consciousness through the feminine element in man, through his anima."[8] Ed Gentry's desire to "penetrate into...unknown territory" is transmitted in precisely this way: through his anima, which, like so many married, middle-aged men, he projects onto a younger woman. On the day before the canoe trip, returning from his lunch with Lewis, Drew and Bobby, Ed walks into his studio, where a pretty, young model is posing for a panties ad, and suddenly finds himself under her spell:

She was somebody I didn't mind looking in the eyes. And straight into them, too, so that if she'd permit it, the look would go deep. I did this, because on the spur of the moment I wanted to. There was a peculiar spot, a kind of tan slice, in her left eye, and it hit me with, I knew right away, strong powers; it was not only recallable, but would come back of itself. . . .

She turned and looked into my face at close range, and the gold-glowing mote fastened on me; it was more gold than any real gold could possibly be; it was alive, and it saw me.[9]

The model has become the carrier of Ed's anima-projection. As such, she is "a bearer of new life"—the psychopomp who opens "the way for him into his own depths."[10] She appears before him on the day of his departure, in the morning, as he makes love to his wife: "It was the heat of another person around me, the moving heat, that brought the image up. The girl from the studio threw back her hair and clasped her breast, and in the center of Martha's heaving and expertly working back, the gold eye shone, not with the practicality of sex, so necessary to its survival, but the promise of it that promised other things, another life, deliverance" (29-30). Thus, the model, as the embodiment of Ed's "soul-image," impels him toward a spiritual rebirth. "The anima," writes Erich Neumann, "is the vehicle par excellence of the transformative character. It is the mover, the instigator of change, whose fascination drives, lures, and encourages the male to all the adventures of the soul and spirit, of action and creation in the inner and the outward world."[11]

For Ed to achieve true psychological maturity, however, he must ultimately, in the language of analytical psychology, "detach" his anima-projection from the model and come to recognize that the magical feminine power he perceives in her is actually a force that resides within himself. As Gerhard Adler observes, once the shadow has been assimilated in the course of the individuation process, "future development [must] go in the direction of a withdrawal of projection, of an internalization of the anima."[12] This is precisely the direction that Gentry's inner development takes. By the close of the novel, he is able to say of the model that "she is imaginary" (235)—i.e., a function of his imagination, of his own psyche. The "magic" he had once seen in her eyes he now recognizes as belonging to "the night river"—to his unconscious, to that immanent power which runs "nowhere but in my head" and which "underlies, in one way or another, everything I do" (234). And the result of this recognition is that Ed now has direct and unobstructed access to the creative springs within him. He no longer feels compelled to seek the mysterious, life-enhancing energy in the outer world, in nature or in other women. Rather, he realizes that this elemental force, symbolized by the river, belongs to *him*: "in me it still is, and will be until I die, green, rocky, deep, fast, slow, and beautiful beyond reality" (234).

Deliverance, then, presents a picture of a man who, by establishing a creative connection with the feminine side of his psyche, experiences a psychic rebirth, an expansion of his personality, including his artistic powers. The anima, in this book, is shown in her positive guise: as the muse, the *femme inspiratrice,* who, like Dante's Beatrice, leads man toward spiritual fulfillment.

For the most part, however, popular culture does not dwell on this aspect of the anima archetype. Reflecting the patriarchal attitude which pervades Western culture—and which regards the feminine world of the psyche with anxiety and distrust—most popular works portray the anima very negatively: as succubus rather than psychopomp. The sinister "she-creatures" which haunt the myths of the world—the sirens, Circes, nixies, night-hags, Lorelei, lamia, poison damsels and other female fantasy figures who embody man's primitive fear of the feminine—have taken up their residence, like the other early gods of legend and lore, in the popular arts, in movies, best-sellers, TV shows and comic books.

This fact is make strikingly clear by one series of comic books in particular: the *Conan the Barbarian* comics published by Stan Lee's Marvel Group and based on the fiction of Robert E. Howard, a prolific writer of action stories for the "pulp" magazines of the 1930s. Though he turned out stories in a variety of genres—Western, detective, ghost, sport, oriental-adventure—he is best remembered today for his "sword-and-sorcery" fiction: lurid fantasies, set in dark, imaginary worlds and starring "brawny barbarians" who, with battle ax or broad sword in hand (and scantily clad "slave wenches" clinging helplessly to their sides), hack and cleave their way through legions of supernatural foes.

Given the he-man quality of his fiction, it is worth noting that Howard lived with his parents all his life and was—in the words of fellow fantasy writer L. Sprague de Camp—"excessively devoted" to his mother, who, in her early sixties, developed terminal cancer.[13] The day before her death, Howard visited her in the hospital. Upon hearing from a nurse that his mother had no chance of recovery, the thirty-year-old author went to his car, took a pistol from the glove compartment, and shot himself in the head. Howard's clearly pathological, ultimately fatal, attachment to his mother may also help explain the prevalence of seductive but extremely dangerous women in his work. It is a rare issue of *Conan* that does not contain at least one bad anima figure. Some typical story titles from the comic book series (which includes *Conan the Barbarian;* a large format magazine called *The Savage Sword of Conan;* and a "spin-off" title based on another of Howard's creations, *Red Sonja)* are: "The Warrior and the Were-Woman," "Men Call Her Wolf-Woman," "The Sorceress of the Swamp," "Web of the Spider Queen," and "Slave of the Amazon Queen." The blurb on the back cover of a recent collection of early *Conan the Barbarian* comic book stories clearly reveals their fixation on the figure of the *femme fatale:* "In thief-infested Zamora, Conan the Barbarian battles wizards and warriors—and *women* more dangerous than either!"[14]

Perhaps the most sinister "she-creature" in all of the Conan comic books appears in a story entitled "The Flame Winds of Lost Khitai" (*Conan* no. 32). Toward the end of this tale, the barbarian hero follows an enticing blonde into a bottomless pool. As they dive deep into the "watery blackness," the "sloe-eyed wench" turns toward the hero and wraps him in her arms—whereupon she abruptly changes into a "creature spawned in some nether hell": a loathsome thing with the head of a woman and the body of an octopus. Enclosed in her tentacles, Conan can only stare into her eyes—"eyes not really those of even a half-woman, but of some monster which has assumed human form to ensnare him." Finally, the Cimmerian manages to close "his mind to the image of haunting deadly beauty," free his sword arm, and slice off her head.[15] This hypnotic she-creature, whose power nearly pulls Conan into a watery grave, has many mythological cousins—the sirens, the Lorelei, the Rusalka, the nixies—lovely water-spirits whose songs lure men to their deaths:

> Half she drew him down,
> Half sank he down
> And nevermore was seen.[16]

Of all negative anima images, however, the most terrifying is undoubtedly the devouring woman, the supernatural female whose ravenous sexual appetite literally drains men dry and whose symbol is the bloody mouth, bristling with teeth (in psychoanalytic terms, an "upward displacement" of the fantasy image of the *vagina dentata).* This nightmare creature is very old, appearing in the ancient Middle East, for instance, in the figure of Lilith, the "Queen of the demons," who, according to Hebrew legend, was Adam's first wife. Refusing to lie beneath her mate during the sexual act because she would not assume such a submissive position, she deserted him. "Adam complained to God, who sent three angels, named Sanvi, Sansavi, and Semangalef, to bring her back. They found her beside the Red Sea, where she was coupling with lascivious demons and giving birth to a brood of demonic children called *lilin* or *liliot* at the rate of a hundred a day. The angels told her to return to Adam, but she refused...." Lilith became "the night hag," the "terror by night," who "preyed on newly born babies" and "attacked men who were sleeping alone, seducing them in their dreams and sucking their blood."[17]

The descendants of Lilith in myth and literature include the medieval succubus—the female demon who lies with mortal men in the dark, draining them of their will and vitality—and later, in the nineteenth century, the *femme fatale,* with her raven black hair, deathly pale complexion, and (to quote a line from Swinburne's poem "Dolores") "cruel red mouth like a venemous flower." In our own time, this terrifying phantasm appears almost exclusively in the popular arts, where she generally takes the form of the vampire woman, the Bride of Dracula. Though countless horror films and comic books have featured her, Stoker's original novel remains the most powerful portrayal of the vampire-woman in popular art, perfectly capturing the frightening, transfixing eroticism which is the essence of this creature. In the following passage, for instance, young Jonathan Harker, who is being held captive in the castle of Dracula, awakens to find three beautiful women—the brides of the vampire count—in the darkness of his chamber:

All three had brilliant white teeth that shone like pearls against the ruby of their voluptuous lips.... I felt in my heart a wicked, burning desire that they would kiss me with those lips.

*   *   *

I lay quiet, looking out under my eyelashes in an agony of delightful anticipation. The fair girl advanced and bent over me till I could feel the movement of her breath upon me....I was afraid to raise my eyelids but looked out and saw perfectly under the lashes. The girl was on her knees, and bent over me, simply gloating. There was a delightful voluptuousness which was both thrilling and repulsive, and as she arched her neck, she actually licked her lips like an animal....I closed my eyes in a langorous ecstasy and waited—waited with beating heart.[18]

The female vampire, however, is not always an actual bloodsucker and man-eater. Often, the negative anima is portrayed as vampiric, not in a physical, but in a spiritual or psychic sense: a woman who drains men of their souls, turning them into slaves, clowns or mindless beasts. This is the figure of "La Belle Dame sans Merci"—The Beautiful Lady without Pity— whose mythic progenitor is the ancient Greek sorceress Circe. Contemporary incarnations of this archetypal image can be found all the time in the popular arts, from the "soaps"—where she generally appears as a heartless homewrecker or sexually competitive "career woman"—to hit songs like the Everly Brothers rock 'n' roll classic "Cathy's Clown," in which she takes the form of a pretty teenage tease who makes her boy friends into buffoons. The Circe figure is also a favorite subject of country-western musicians. In the country hit "Bandy the Rodeo Clown," for example, the singer tells the sad (and familiar) story of a rugged rodeo star—"a bull hookin' son-of-a-gun"—who "was ridin' high till a pretty girl rode him to the ground." Once a first-class bronc-buster who was "closin' in on number one," he is now a pathetic figure, a drunken rodeo clown who keeps the crowds entertained between the "ropin' and ridin' " events.[19]

This song is a kind of country music version of what is undoubtedly the most powerful representation of the negative anima archetype in all the popular arts: Josef von Sternberg's *The Blue Angel.* Though he doesn't mention it by name, Jung himself seems to have this movie in mind when he describes the way in which the anima sometimes makes itself felt in a man's life:

It is no use at all to learn a list of archetypes by heart. Archetypes are complexes of experience that come upon us like fate, and their effects are felt in our most personal life. The anima no longer crosses our path as a goddess, but, it may be, as an intimately personal misadventure, or perhaps as our best venture. When, for instance, a highly esteemed professor in his seventies abandons his family and runs off with a young red-headed actress, we know that the gods have claimed another victim.[20]

I intend, in the remaining pages of this section, to discuss *The Blue Angel* in some detail, and to compare it to another movie with which it would seem to have little in common: *Saturday Night Fever*. Despite the artistic gap which separates these two films—in terms of their aesthetic qualities, there *is* no comparison between Sternberg's brilliantly wrought study and the raucous, rough-edged disco movie—they do share certain themes and motifs. Both are seemingly naturalistic portraits of men who escape from the constrictions of their workaday lives into enticing, somewhat forbidden night worlds, represented in the one case by the cabaret, in the other by the discotheque. More significantly, beneath the surface realism of these movies lies a similar level of symbolic meaning; for the psychological theme of both, I believe, is the confrontation between masculine ego-consciousness and the archetypal feminine. The different responses which the two male protagonists have to their animas, and the different fates these characters meet, tell us a great deal, not only about our culture's shifting attitudes toward the feminine, but also about the way in which popular art operates symbolically to foster psychic integration.

The protagonist of *The Blue Angel* is Immanuel Rath, a middle-aged professor of English at the local boy's high school, whose controlled, rigidly organized character—the kind psychoanalysis would define as "anal erotic"—is made immediately and strikingly clear. We first meet him on a typical morning as his landlady, in what is obviously a well-established routine, sets out his breakfast and calls him to the table. Rath (played by the great German actor Emil Jannings) is a large, imposing man, meticulous in dress and appearance. He is also pompous and somewhat priggish. Sitting in the sunlit room, surrounded by books, he pours his coffee with a prim little gesture—his pinky-finger cocked at precisely the right angle—which perfectly captures his stiffly formal, fastidious nature. His life, it is clear, is strictly circumscribed; the world he inhabits is one of extreme respectability, rationality and order, with little room in it for emotion and none at all for passion.

When he goes to feed his canary a bit of sugar, he finds the bird lying dead on the bottom of its cage, and gently lifts it out, staring at it in shock and bewilderment. His landlady—a down-to-earth, indeed rather coarse, woman—walks over, plucks the carcass from his hand, and tosses into the nearby stove. The look of incomprehension and dismay on Rath's face as he seats himself again at the table contrasts sharply with the landlady's unsentimental treatment of the dead bird.

Unlike the woman, Rath, it is clear, has a strong streak of sentimentality in him: a common characteristic in fiercely controlled, hyperintellectual men, whose repressed, underdeveloped emotional sides will often manifest themselves in bouts of mawkishness. Moreover, it is also clear from his reaction to the canary's death that there is a dark, disorderly, earthy side of existence which Rath knows very little about (again, unlike the landlady, who takes it so for granted that she doesn't think twice about it). And it is precisely his ignorance of this realm—which is the realm not only of death but of life, which is to say, the chthonic realm of the Great Mother, of the dark energies of nature—which makes Rath so vulnerable. For as we have seen in the case of the shadow, the powers we are most unconscious of are the ones we are most susceptible to, most likely to be consumed by. As Jung warns,

if you take a typical intellectual who is terribly afraid of falling in love, you will think him very foolish. But he is most probably right, because he will very likely make foolish nonsense when he falls in love. He will be caught most certainly, because his feeling only reacts to an archaic and dangerous type of woman. This is why intellectuals are inclined to marry beneath them. They are caught by the landlady perhaps, or by the cook, because they are unaware of their archaic feeling through which they get caught. But they are right to be afraid because...in their feeings they can be influenced, they can be caught, they can be cheated, and they know it. Therefore never force a man into his feelings when he is an intellectual. He controls it was an iron hand because it is very dangerous.[21]

It is not the landlady who catches Rath, however, but a different type of "archaic and dangerous" woman. Patrolling his classroom during an exam, the professor spies a student peeking at a postcard of a sexy cabaret singer named Lola Lola, who is appearing at a local club, The Blue Angel. Soon after this scene, the film cuts to the nightclub itself. We see Lola's face, framed by a cheap backdrop of fake, flickering sunrays; cardboard clouds dance on wires, while a grotesque cherub flutters its wings. The tacky celestial scenery surrounding Lola makes her look like a fallen angel. As she struts across the stage or poses, hands on hips, legs astride, in silk stockings and merry widow corset, she is the epitome of the blatantly sexual, cinematic vamp.

Seeking out several of his most wayward students—who have taken to hanging around Lola's dressing room—Rath journeys to The Blue Angel that night. The scene is brilliantly shot. The seamy and sinister section of town he furtively wanders through—with its swirling mists, crooked streets and grotesque, expressionistically distorted buildings (reminiscent of another masterwork of the German cinema, *The Cabinet of Dr. Caligari*)—is clearly a kind of dreamscape, a representation of a dark, previously unexplored part of Rath's own psyche. This ominous city of night, in short—which contrasts so sharply with the strictly disciplined, sunlit world of the classroom he inhabits during the day—symbolizes the forbidden shadow-realm which lurks beneath Rath's irreproachable public persona and into which he is now being lured for the first time by the siren-song of the archetypal anima.

Once inside The Blue Angel, Rath is completely at a loss. The epitome of authority and dignity in the classroom, he is, in this disreputable but titillating world, clumsy and confused. Standing in Lola's dressing room—with performers constantly rushing in and out—he is always getting in the way and tripping over things. He sweats, puffs, stammers and at one point, later on, swoons from excitement. When Lola, standing a few feet away from him, changes from one revealing costume into another, he does not know where to look, averting his eyes but stealing guilty glances at her exposed flesh. "You've been bewitching my students," he reprimands her, mustering his authorty. She shatters his hauteur with a smirk. If you are a professor, she chides, in her seductive, slightly mocking voice, you should know enough to remove your hat in the presence of a lady. The blustering, overbearing Rath is instantly reduced to a childlike state of embarrassment and confusion as he fumbles for his hat. The professor, it is clear, is completely out of his element in this shady if intoxicating world. It is Lola who is headmaster here, Rath the bungling, self-conscious student.

This reversal of roles is typical of anima stories, since the anima-figure often has a great aura of wisdom and experience about her. H. Rider Haggard's She, for example, is known as "Wisdom's Daughter,"[22] Hawthorne's Beatrice Rappaccini is reputedly "qualified to fill a professor's chair,"[23] and Poe's Ligeia is a woman remarkable for both her extraordinary learning and colossal will power. As the personification of the *Eros* principle, the anima possesses a profound knowledge of the body, of relationships, of the sexual and emotional realm, which the hyperrational hero, who is all *Logos*, completely lacks.

Rath meets several other characters in Lola's dressing room, characters who, like the singer herself, function both realistically—as true-to-life portraits of the denizens of a sleazy 1930s German cabaret—and symbolically, as the dream-figures Rath encounters during his descent into a dark, psychic underworld. There is Kiefert, the fat, oily manager of the company, who identifies himself as a Professor of Magic and therefore regards Rath as a confrere. A charlatan and toady, he is Rath's shadow-figure, the disreputable, self-serving alter ego of the high-minded pedagogue. There is another figure who wanders through this scene: a wasted clown, a mute, unsettling specter who stares at Rath with haunted, unfathomable eyes. There is something ominous about him; and, in fact, he is, as we are soon to find out, an omen: a warning, like the pale victims of Keats' "La Belle Dame sans Merci" or the swine in Circe's pigsty, of the dangers of getting too close to the negative anima.

Rath, however, cannot stay away. "You've come back," Lola says when he appears in her room the following evening. "They always do." Within seconds, she has him completely in her power. He sits at her dressing table while she applies make-up. His chair is much lower than hers, so that even though he is far bigger than she, Lola is above, looking down on him—a position symbolic of her total dominance. She hands him her make-up case to hold. Rath is pleased, flattered by her attention, though his half playful, half gallant service will soon enough turn into something close to real slavery. Lola takes a cigarette and, as she turns to hand Rath the case, deliberately drops it. Rath falls to his knees and scrambles under the table for the cigarettes: in the space of a very few moments, Lola has succeeded in getting the dignified professor to crawl at her feet. When he emerges seconds later, disheveled, she leans down, holds his face with one hand and brushes his hair like a mother preparing her baby for his first day at school. "Now go to work," she says, and hands him her powder box. She teases him, making him blush like a schoolboy by telling him how good-looking he is. All at once, she turns and blows the powder into his face. He chokes, coughs, while she, with mock contrition, brushes him off and strokes his chin, making him squirm with delight.

When Lola goes onstage to perform, Kiefert takes Rath to a box seat and proudly introduces the honored professor to the audience. This scene occurs at the end of the first half of the film. At the end of the second half, the magician will again introduce Rath to the crowd assembled in the club—but under horribly different circumstances. At this point, Rath is in seventh heaven. As Lola sings "Falling In Love Again" to him from the stage, he blushes and beams, and—suddenly conscious of his exposed position—glances embarrasedly around him. Directly below him is a carved wooden ship's figurehead of a wild-haired siren with naked, jutting breasts—a mythic representation of the power which now has Rath in its grasp.

His fall, from this point on, is swift and terrifying. The following morning, Rath arrives at his classroom late, having spent the night in Lola's bed. His students—some of whom had witnessed his unseemly behavior in the singer's dressing room the previous evening—greet him with howls of derision, catcalls, contemptuous cries of "Unrath! Unrath!" (the German word for "garbage"). The blackboards are covered with cruel, insulting caricatures. Rath's loss of control over the students he once tyrannized represents his loss of control over his own tightly-reined, long-repressed emotions, which have suddenly run away with him. He leaves his job and proposes to Lola. At their wedding party, Kiefert entertains the guests by performing some of his crude prestidigitation, producing an egg from behind the bridegroom's ear. Rath crows like a rooster with pride and pleasure. It is another moment that will be repeated near the end of the movie—though, again, with a terrible difference.

During what seems to be their honeymoon, Rath accidentally drops one of Lola's suitcases upon the floor. Out spill hundreds of pin-up pictures, which Lola sells to make extra money. Rath is outraged. He won't have his wife's photograph peddled to the drunken, leering customers. "Not while I have a cent!" he proclaims. The scene fades out. When the next scene fades in, we see that a horrible transformation has taken place. Rath—whom a moment ago we saw in his prime, a proud, prosperous, vigorous man—now sits hunched over a table, looking haggard and seedy. A cigarette butt hangs from his slack lips and the hair of this once meticulous man is matted and disarrayed. Slowly he rises from his chair and begins to drift hopelessly from table to table, a trayful of his wife's pin-up pictures in his hand.

In Lola's dressing room, the once-obsequious Kiefert contemptuously tells Rath that he might sell more pictures if he took a shave. After Kiefert leaves, Rath shakes with rage, self-loathing and despair. "Better to die like a dog than live such a life!" he cries, and rushes out of the room. Lola sits undisturbed by her dressing table, her long legs casually crossed. Clearly, she understands her hold on Rath—knows that he is her slave, that she has him completely in her power. A moment later, the door opens and Rath enters abjectly, shoulders bowed, head bent low. "My stockings," she commands, moving over to the couch. He drops to his knees and begins to roll her stockings up her legs. A bell, a timer, rings. "Curling iron!" she snaps. He leaps up to fetch it and brings it to her. "Too hot!" she scolds. He obediently runs over to a calendar tacked onto the wall and starts to cool the iron by pressing it against the pages of the calendar. Days, months, and years go up in smoke.

When we next meet Rath, the sight is almost too grotesque and painful to bear. Looking gaunt and horribly grubby, he sits before a make-up mirror applying the same greasepaint, bulbous nose and fright-wig worn by the earlier clown, the specter who haunted Lola's dressing room at the start of the film. The immense clown's collar he places over his head looks like a yoke. Rath has taken his place in the long line of Lola's victims, of men she has ensnared, degraded and finally ruined. The ultimate humiliation, however, is yet to come. The manager has booked the troupe back into The Blue Angel and his advertised Professor Immanuel Rath as the headliner of the show. Rath is forced to appear onstage in front of his former neighbors, colleagues and students, dressed in his grotesque buffoon's outfit, while Kiefert tries to get laughs by cracking eggs on the old man's head and making him cock-a-doodle-doo like a rooster. Lola, meanwhile, stands backstage, embracing a new, young lover.

Driven to the end of his sanity, Rath goes berserk and tries to murder Lola. He is subdued and strapped into a straitjacket, from which the suddenly sympathetic Kiefert releases him. Rath stumbles through the darkness and makes his way back to his old classroom, where he dies slumped over his desk. The final shot of the movie shows Lola onstage, sitting astride a chair and singing "Falling In Love Again." It is significant that, though years have passed since she last performed at The Blue Angel—a period of time which has seen Rath degenerate from a proud, robust man into a shabby, pathetic ruin—Lola looks as young and voluptuous as she did in the beginning. "The anima," writes Frieda Fordham, "has a timeless quality—she often looks young, though there is always the suggestion of years of experience behind her."[24]

On the one hand, then, *The Blue Angel* can be viewed as the representation of a typical masculine nightmare-image: the fatal woman who maintains her beauty and vitality by draining the life and soul from her male lovers. Seen in this light, the movie takes on the aspect of a neurotic symptom. We may be tempted to condemn it for perpetuating an invidious male myth, to dismiss it as nothing more than the product of a pathological culture which hates and fears women. And in fact there is some truth to this charge. According to analytical psychology, however, every neurosis has a positive aspect. As Frieda Fordham points out, Jung holds that a neurotic symptom is not just the manifestation of a disease but "an attempt to compensate for a one-sided attitude to life, and a voice, as it were, drawing attention to a side of [the] personality that has been neglected or repressed."[25]

Edward C. Whitmont, for example, describes the case of a businessman characterized by his "controlled rationality" and rejection of emotional values. This individual was seeking psychiatric aid because he suffered from a severe foot fetish, an inability to function sexually without first licking the toes of a female. Interpreted symbolically, this symptom revealed itself as an urge to worship at the feet of women—i.e., as a compensatory attempt by the unconscious to correct the ego's one-sided orientation by forcing it to glorify the neglected realm of the feminine. Once this meaning was made conscious—once the individual recognized his "perversion" as an extreme effort by the unconscious to draw attention to an area of the personality that required development—the compulsion to "act out" the symbolic meaning of the impulse disappeared.[26] "Thus," writes Jolande Jacobi, "a neurosis can serve as a warning issued by a higher authority, a reminder that our personality is urgently in need of broadening...."[27]

Such a warning, I believe, is precisely the underlying meaning of *The Blue Angel*. When we apply Jung's method of analysis to this movie—that is, when we interpret its characters and actions as *symbols*—we find that, like so much popular art, its real, if unconscious, theme is the integration of the personality; that what it warns men against is not the peril which surrounds seductive women but the peril which results from the overvaluation of (what Erich Neumann calls) "male intellectual consciousness."[28] The symbolic message of *The Blue Angel*, in other words, is not that women are dangerous creatures but that the anima, the feminine side of the male psyche (which is what Lola symbolizes) can, like the shadow or any other element in the unconscious, *become* dangerous if its existence is ignored for too long, if it is too vigorously denied. Rath is undone, not because he comes too close to a sexy female, but because he has never paid any attention to—indeed, has never even acknowledged—the principle of Eros, never made a place for it in his life. And because he has repressed it for so long, he is easily destroyed when it finally rises up and overwhelms him.

A very different fate is met by Tony Manero, the hero of the smash hit movie *Saturday Night Fever*. In an illuminating article on this film, entitled "More Than a Woman: Myth & Mediation in *Saturday Night Fever*," William P. Kelly argues that the central dilemma which the movie sets up and then symbolically resolves is the archetypically American "conflict between community and self-reliance." Tony, as Kelly convincingly shows, is torn between the claims of his Brooklyn neighborhood, which both nourishes and restrains him, and his yearning for the freedom represented by the "Emerald City" of Manhattan. According to Kelly,

like the myths that attenuated the force of primitive man's irreconcilable dilemmas, *Saturday Night Fever* blurs this contradiction through mediation. It effects a reconciliation through the agency of Stephanie Mangano, a mystery woman Tony first sees dancing at 2001. Stephanie is ideally suited to serve as a mediator of Tony's crisis. She transcends all of the polarities the film has carefully established. Both "them" and "us," she is from Brooklyn but lives in Manhattan. She's far more feminine than Annette or the other women of 2001, but she is capable of joining the Faces on an equal footing. Neither cunt nor good girl, she resists all of the compartimentalization that has characterized Tony's previous relationships with women. Finally, and most importantly, she offers Tony community without its attendant restraints.[29]

While Kelly's argument seems impregnable to me, there is, I believe, another symbolic role which Stephanie plays in the film, one suggested by her theme song, "More Than a Woman." Stephanie is Tony's anima. As such, she serves as a mediator of internal as well as external contradictions. The conflict she resolves, in other words, is not only that between the contrasting worlds of Brooklyn and Manhattan, but also that between the opposing psychological poles of Logos and Eros, masculine and feminine. Through Stephanie, Tony is put in touch with feelings of tenderness and friendship he has never experienced before; she is a bridge for him between his tough "macho" persona and his capacity for warmth, softness and sensitivity—"feminine" qualities which, given the rigid sex roles his community lives by, he has always been forced to suppress. (As Kelly notes, Stephanie "embodies the bridge imagery which dominates the film"; and, in fact, the final "bridge" we see in the movie is the one formed by Tony and Stephanie's hands, spanning the screen in a clasp of love and friendship.) When Tony says sarcastically to her near the very start of their relationship, "What do *you* got—a stairway to the stars?" he is speaking more truly than he knows, for Stephanie does indeed turn out to be his "angel of light," who offers him not only liberation from the limitations of Bay Ridge but also redemption from an extremely narrow definition of masculinity.

John Travolta, of course, is the perfect choice for the role of Tony, since he possesses the look of the prototypical street punk and at the same time, as various critics have noted, an odd, androgynous quality. In all his roles—and particularly in the part of "Strip" in the disastrous *Moment by Moment*—he exemplifies what has been called "The New Masculinity." Paul Starr, writing in the *New York Times*, describes the "new masculine hero" as a man who is more "feminine" than the "archetypal old-fashioned" screen heroes like John Wayne and Gary Cooper. "Whereas earlier in this century we were in a 'masculinizing' period—of which [D.H.] Lawrence and Hemingway and the cult of the 'real man' were an expression," writes Starr, "today we are in a period when masculinity is being softened."[30] I agree with Starr that the emergence of this new kind of male hero is a fact of some significance. It is the sign, I think—as is Travolta's tremendous popularity—of a pervasive and extremely important cultural phenomenon which I propose to examine more fully in the following section: a phenomenon which might be called the Return of the Mother.

2

The increasing strength of poetry, defense of earth, and mother consciousness, implies that after hundreds of years of being motionless, the Great Mother is moving again in the psyche. Every day her face becomes clearer.... She is returning, or we are returning to her....

Robert Bly, "I Came Out of the Mother Naked"

Like the shadow, the anima has both a personal and collective aspect. The personal aspect consists of those repressed feminine character traits which every male must raise to consciousness in the course of the individuation process. The collective aspect of the anima is the primordial image of the Feminine, that suprapersonal power symbolized throughout the world by the figure of the Great Mother Goddess, *Magna Mater,* who incarnates the matriarchal spirit.

In his essay "I Came Out of the Mother Naked," the poet Robert Bly, drawing on the work of the Jungian theorist Erich Neumann and the Swiss ethnologist Johann Jakob Bachofen, lyrically defines this spirit, which—using the language of analytical psychology—he calls "Mother consciousness." To him "Matriarchy thinking is intuitive and moves by associative leaps":

When masculine consciousness became aware of itself, it took for its main image the bright blue sky surrounding the sun.... It creates straight roads.... Father consciousness tries to control mammal nature through rules, morality, commandments, and tries to reach spirit through asceticism. The Chinese describe it as the cold, the clear, the south side of the mountain (on which the light always falls), the north side of the river (always in sunlight), the rational, the spirit, the hard.

In mother consciousness there is affection for nature, compassion, love of water, grief and care for the dead, love of whatever is hidden, intuition, ecstasy. The Chinese describe it as the north side of the mountain (always in shadow) and the south side of the river (always in shadow); also as the valley of the world.[31]

Just as every man, in order to be a complete human being, must establish a relationship with his inner femininity, so the spiritual health of any culture requires that both realms of consciousness described by Bly be recognized and revered—brought into balance. But as Erich Neumann pointed out back in 1955, one of Western society's most pernicious problems has been its overvaluation of "father consciousness"—the derogation of the Feminine by an antipathetic patriarchal spirit. "The peril of present-day mankind," writes Neumann in the preface to his classic work, *The Great Mother*, "springs in large part from the one-sidedly patriarchal development of the male intellectual consciousness, which is no longer kept in balance by the matriarchal world of the psyche."[32]

We have already seen that, according to Jung, this kind of psychic one-sidedness brings about a response from the collective unconscious in the form of a compensatory symbol. In the case of the individual, "extreme conscious tendencies" are counterbalanced by fantasy and dream. When the conscious attitude of an entire culture is extremely one-sided, the compensatory archetype will appear in the work of its artists. "Every period has its bias, its particular prejudice, and its psychic malaise," says Jung. "An epoch is like an individual; it has its own limitations of conscious outlook, and therefore requires a compensatory adjustment. This is effected by the collective unconscious when a poet or seer lends expression to the unspoken desire of his times and shows the way, by word or deed, to its fulfillment."[33] Since Jung, as I pointed out earlier, includes both H. Rider Haggard and Sir Arthur Conan Doyle as examples of writers whose work contains such compensatory symbols, it is clear that by "poet or seer" he means the popular artist as well as the "high."

A look at American popular culture of the past ten or twelve years reveals that—undoubtedly as a compensatory response to the "one-sidedly patriarchal" orientation which has always characterized our society—the Great Mother, as Bly claims, has

indeed returned. Considering how long *Magna Mater* was denied
by our culture, it is no wonder that, when she finally *did* reassert
herself, she came back with a vengeance. In the late sixties, the
figure that seemed to dominate America's collective dreams was
the Indian Death-Mother, Kali the Devourer. Kali's emergence
into the forefront of our cultural fantasies could be seen in a kind
of generalized shift of attention away from the female bosom and,
concomitantly, in a growing preoccupation with a very different
feature: the all-consuming mouth. Girlie magazines like *Cavalier,
Rogue,* and *Gent*—all crammed with "buxom beauties"—began
to compete with a host of sex tabloids, most of which dealt
predominantly and quite explicitly with fellatio and cunnilingus,
and tended to treat orality in a blatantly cannibalistic fashion.
"Girl Ghoul Eats Dick for Christmas" is the title of a typical
article in *Screw,* the most commercially successful of all the porno
papers,[34] and *Eat* (one of the sleazier and shorter-lived) featured a
pair of fat, drooling lips as its logo and had for a mascot, not a
fertile bunny, but a naked woman, tongue hanging hungrily from
her lips, devouring a plateful of male genitalia.

The same phenomenon was evident in porno films. *The
Immoral Mr. Tease,* the most famous of Russ Meyer's bare breast
extravaganzas, was, for many years, the highest grossing "blue
movie" ever made; but *Deep Throat,* a film starring a young lady
capable of—in the words of one ecstatic reviewer—"engulf[ing]
stiff dicks right down to the balls" ("They simply disappear into
her mouth. . . . Such a display of cock-consumption has rarely, if
ever, been recorded on the. . . movie screen"),[35] set new box-office
records, grossing millions of dollars within months of its release.
And the songs of Grace Slick, lead singer of the popular rock
group The Jefferson Airplane, who declared her role as Good
Mother of the counterculture by giving birth, after a well-
publicized pregnancy, to a child she originally planned to name
"god," suddenly shifted from flower-power fantasies to visions of
cannibal orgies. "You could learn to dine on your friends," the
singer tells us in "Silver Spoon." "Pour their bones into a
cannibal soup / Muscles like steer, bones like wine."

In the late 1960s, interestingly, the figure of Kali, the Terrible
Mother, seemed to surface first in the dreams of the
counterculture. At the peak of their popularity, for example, the
Rolling Stones adopted for a trademark a pair of thick red lips

with a fat tongue thrust out from between them—an obvious caricature of Mick Jagger's own famous liver lips, but also (as the Stones themselves were well aware), the emblem of Kali.[36] The androgynous Jagger became the cannibal queen, and the counterculture, fast in the grip of the Teeth Mother, worshipped him: the Stones' emblem began popping up everywhere—on watches, key rings, pins, pendants, patches, T-shirts, belt buckles. At the same time, the songs of other rock musicians began to reflect a fascination with the Cannibal Goddess. Alice Cooper, the man-hag superstar, rose to prominence by singing about "Dead Babies," butchering live chickens and baby dolls on stage, and—like Hecate, "the snake-entwined moon-goddess of ghosts and the dead"[37]—performing with a live python coiled around his body. The cover of the first album by a group called Mom's Apple Pie depicted a sinister young lady smacking her lips over a dripping flesh pie, while T. Rex crooned to a girlfriend, "You got the teeth of the hydra upon you."[38]

The rise of the Terrible Mother within the counterculture was also reflected in its other characteristic popular art form, the underground comic. By the early 1970s, the "New Comix," which were once an expression of the same psychedelic-flower child consciousness that created acid rock and love-ins, were almost exclusively horror-porn productions, dominated by the figure of the Devouring Woman. A classic example is Richard Corben's "Gastric Fortitude" from *Death Rattle* no. 1 (now a collector's item). In it, a young man seeks shelter from a storm in a Gothic castle inhabited by a svelte beauty who, when the hero removes his wet clothing, tells him that he looks "good enough to eat"— and then proceeds quite literally to devour him. Even the comics of Robert Crumb, which, in earlier days, were filled entirely with such benign creations as Fritz the Cat, Flakey Foont and Mr. Natural, began to abound in Terrible Mother figures, like the razor-beaked "vulture demonesses" who capture Eggs Ackley in *Big Ass Comics* (fig. 2).

But if the Devouring Mother appeared first in underground places—in the porn-rags of America's sexual subculture and the anti-establishment "comix" of the young—her image soon emerged into the cultural mainstream. The primal fear which the movie *Jaws*, for example, served to arouse in so many millions of viewers (and then, through the depiction of the monster's

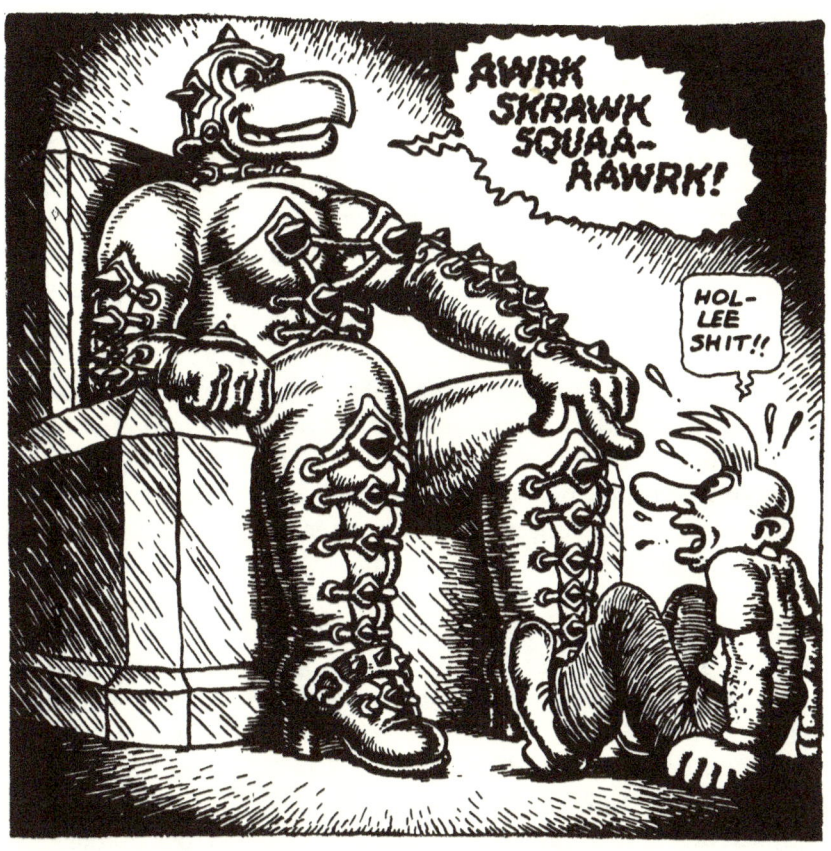

destruction, to assuage) was that of the *vagina dentata*.[39] The image of the Terrible Mother also lies behind one of the most popular cinematic genres of the 1970s—the disaster movie. Ever since these films became popular, they have been condemned by critics, not merely as bad movies but as symptoms of something deeply disturbing in the American character. Their appeal has been attributed to various forms of morbidity, from sheer sadism to an intensely pathological puritanism which revels in the sight of sexually permissive communities destroyed by retributive powers.[40] While I have no intention of defending disaster films as examples of cinematic art, I do believe that, for all their fascination with carnage and catastrophe, they actually serve a constructive, *corrective* purpose, analogous to the psychological function of *The Blue Angel*. For, just as the underlying theme of von Sternberg's movie is that, unless a man learns to value his own inner femininity, he is likely to come to a very bad end, so the symbolic meaning of disaster movies is that the culture as a whole must come to terms with the Feminine, or else suffer the disastrous consequences.

First, I define disaster movie as a film whose *raison d'etre* is the portrayal of a catastrophe involving the spectacular destruction of some colossal human creation (skyscraper, jumbo jet, ocean liner, city) and the mass of humanity inhabiting it. A movie can contain a disaster without being a disaster movie. *Gone With the Wind* is a good example. While the burning of Atlanta is a highlight of the film, it is not what the picture is about. Similarly, large-scale slaughter alone does not make a disaster movie. More humans are killed in *The Wild Bunch* than in *The Towering Inferno* and *Airport '77* combined. In disaster films, however, people do not die at the hands of their fellow men but as a result of being trapped in a place (or thing) that is either sinking, crumbling, burning or exploding.

What *does* cause the destruction in disaster movies? Here, I believe, is the key to their meaning. The "classic" disaster films are *The Poseidon Adventure* (in which a titanic luxury liner is capsized by a tidal wave); the *Airport* series (in the most recent of which a 747 crashes into the ocean after passing through the Bermuda triangle); *Earthquake* and *The Towering Inferno* (or "Shake and Bake," as *Variety* dubbed them; in which, respectively, Los Angeles is devasted by a monstrous quake and the world's tallest skyscraper is gutted by a twelve-alarm blaze). What strikes me as especially significant about these movies is that, in each of them, the agent of destruction is one of the four basic elements:

Earth	*Earthquake*
Air	*the Airport* pictures
Fire	*The Towering Inferno*
Water	*The Poseidon Adventure*

In short, the common denominator among all these films—the central situation or fantasy which they depict—is the destruction of some supreme technological achievement (an unsinkable ship, a fireproof building, a mammoth airplane, a metropolis) by the natural world.

What is the meaning of this fantasy? It seems to me that the message which disaster movies convey, by symbolic means, to the viewer's unconscious is that what technology has done to nature, to the world of the Mother, is immoral; that, in certain essential respects, our way of life is a violation of the principle she represents; and that if we continue to do violence to her, we will draw down (and *deserve*) a fierce retribution. As I have said, the spiritual well-being of every society (as of every individual) requires the union of patriarchal and matriarchal modes of consciousness—father thinking and mother thinking, in Bly's terms. The disaster movie—appearing at a moment when matriarchal consciousness, in the form of the modern feminist movement, was starting to make itself strongly felt in our society—serves as a warning from the depths of the collective unconscious (as projected into popular art, the expression of our cultural dreams) of the ecological and *psycho*logical damage which results when the powers of *Magna Mater* are disdained.

Seen in this light, the disaster movie is just one part of that pervasive cultural phenomenon Bly describes as the return of the Mother. Like the personal anima, *Magna Mater* possesses both a negative and positive aspect, symbolized respectively by Kali, the Cannibal Goddess, and Demeter, Mother of Life and New Birth. While the negative face of the Mother showed itself first in our society—inevitably, perhaps, since chaos always precedes cosmos—we have since entered a period dominated more by Demeter. The most striking sign of the rise of the Good Mother is our current obsession with nature: our growing ambivalence about the products of the patriarchal mind—about the value of unbridled technological development—and a concurrent glorification of Mother Earth. Despite the faddish and commercial aspects of the back-to-nature movement (every item on the market seems to be "natural" these days—the label is, apparently, a guarantee of success; it's very much like the situation in the schlock-art houses, where every cheap reproduction is proclaimed an "original"), the desire to be surrounded by greenery instead of machinery reflects, I believe, a genuine revival of the matriarchal spirit. When large numbers of people begin talking to their plants, the Good Mother is really making herself felt.

This new reverence for the Great Mother Goddess can be seen in the work of many feminist writers. A recent issue of *Heresies: A*

Feminist Publication on Art and Politics, for example, is devoted
entirely to meditations on the meaning of the Great Goddess for
modern women. Its contents include Merlin Stone's "The Three
Faces of Goddess Spirituality," Carol P. Christ's "Why Women
Need the Goddess," Martha Alsup's "Finding the Goddess:
Finding Myself," and many other essays, poems and graphics, all
in praise of the *Magna Mater* archetype.

Typical of this revival of interest in the Great Mother
Goddess is the work of the popular novelist and poet Daniela
Gioseffi, whose work not only celebrates the return of Demeter but
is itself an interesting sign of that return. In an essay on the
origin of the belly dance—which she sees as a debased form of a
matriarchal birth rite and performs as a "joyous tribute" to the
Mother, a celebration of female potency—Gioseffi insists that
women's liberation must not be "a movement toward a greater
patriarchal despotism for *both* sexes, but a revival of the
archetypal female consciousness as giver of life, nurturer of
living things, and maker of life-giving arts."[42] Accordingly, she
associates herself throughout her poetry not with the negative
aspect of the Feminine—phallic-aggressive, man-eating—but
with its creative and regenerative side. In "My Venus Fly Trap is
Dying," for example, the poet recoils from the carnivorous plant,
the *vagina dentata* of the vegetable world, and identifies herself
with the tree, the symbol, according to Jungian psychology, of
psychic synthesis, of growth toward a higher, more unified state
of being:

> I've loved and envied plants
> for their peacefulness,
> their quiet conversion of the sun,
> that first all contingent link
> between solar energy and animal.
>
> But this Venus Fly Trap
> is too much for me
> named by men
> with the word "Vanity."
>
> It will have to die
> and be tossed into the waste can
> with the bright red lipstick

I no longer wear
and the blood red nail polish
I've given up.

This Venus Fly Trap
doesn't photosynthesize
quite peacefully enough.
It's trying to become an animal
And I
trying so hard to become a tree
can't bear it.[43]

Gioseffi, in short, does not imagine herself as one of the Furies, a disintegrator of the male ego. Renouncing the role of feminist avenger, she calls instead for a new *integration*. The image of woman as life-bearer dominates her poems, and the procreative power she exalts in them is spiritual as well as physical: works like "Eggs," "The Vases of Wombs," "Caves," "Birth Dance, Belly Dancer," are paeans to the birth of the feminine soul in American society. At the same time they point to the need for psychic totality, for the union of Logos and Eros in the human personality, and suggest the perils of suppression. Though "Nippled Trees Outlast an Age of Iron" is, on its most literal level, a poem about ecology, it also symbolizes a dangerous psychological situation: the inner damage that results when the "male intellectual consciousness" denies the "matriarchal world of the psyche":

You dreamed of keeping her
a wife in a pumpkin shell,
but no cave holds the sea.

When you tied down her hair with steel cables
and cemented it in concrete,
she sent up an unpredictable hurricane.

Her hair flies in your face and blinds you.
She floods you with birth,
riddles your sleep with a woman's intuition.

For Gioseffi, then, the essential human task is self-realization: redemption *can* be achieved, her poems tell us, but only when the masculine and feminine are allied in each psyche. Her most jubilant poems envision this wholeness. "Paradise Is Not a Place" and "To My Androsphinx" are boisterous love songs—lusty, profane. The union they celebrate, though, is not merely sexual, for the dominant image in each is the syzygy, the symbol of psychic conjunction:

> Our body melts into one huge pink rock,
> my penis now in your mouth,
> your clitoris in my pupil.
> We are a Magritte mountain floating out to sea,
> adrift in the Atlantic,
> circumnavigating the world like an explorer's ship
> until it settles in the blue Pacific.
>
> Sailors point and say: "There's GREAT MOUNT
> ANDROGYNOUS,
> once a fornicating woman and man,
> now turned into a pink mountain!"
> Missionaries plant a neon cross on top
> to mark the spot
> where the penis merged with the clitoris
> and the world is at peace in the clouds
> with gulls flapping gently at its peak.

The note of serenity on which this poem ends is significant, for, ultimately, all of Gioseffi's poetry works toward harmony and peace, toward the reconciliation of the sexes and of the sexual opposites within each human being (the two goals, of course, are finally the same, the first growing out of the second). Her poems ask men to recognize their own repressed feminity, to rediscover their own inner Eros. For Women, they are reminders of a primordial connection with earth and with life—a connection which must be preserved if feminism is to hold its own against the patriarchal spirit and turn us away from technocracy.

"I have a pleasant dream," says the poet in "Peace Prospect,"

> of a land inhabited only by bright animals
> who refuse fire
> and eat nothing but leaves.
> I count the people I have tried to touch
> and my hands melt sand into glass.
> There is no chance between us for a fine love.

We can't manufacture food like vegetation
standing in the light.
Photosynthesis is the trees making love with the sun.
A vague intuition blossoms in my stomach.
We are a mind-ridden race and incompatible with earth.
A better race will come.
I feel bright animals waiting in my genes
for the right moment.

By the end of this poem, the identification between the author and the Mother is complete. It is Demeter who speaks to us in the last few lines, and—as we would expect in one of Gioseffi's poems—it is a new birth that she foretells: the birth of a "better race," of a healthier, more balanced society. In his essay on "Psychology and Literature," Jung says that "whenever the collective unconscious becomes a living experience and is brought to bear upon the conscious outlook of an age, this event is a creative act which is of importance to everyone." Thus, Gioseffi's poems fulfill the function of all archetypal art, both popular and high, for a primordial figure—the Good Mother Goddess—is present throughout them, holding out the promise of a new and higher order.

Chapter Five

Hero With 2000 Faces

1

PETE THE PLUMBER is in sorry shape. Unhappy at home, where he and his shrewish wife bicker incessantly, and fed up with his filthy, unfulfilling job, he is close to despair. "Always tryin' t' make ends meet," he cries in frustration as he stares at a mountainous pile of bills. "And for what?"

And then the final straw: his perky little companion, Plungo ("The Plumber's Friend"), an anthropomorphic toilet bowl plunger, comes running in to show his boss the headline in the evening newspaper: "WOMAN STRANGLED BY HER OWN TOILET; Plumber Sought by Police." It seems that a customer of Pete's, testing out a toilet bowl our hero had repaired that very afternoon, has been sucked inside and suffocated. The plumber yields to despair. "There's only one thing to do," he mutters, and heads for the bathroom. He climbs inside the toilet bowl, bids the cruel world good-bye, pulls on the lever, and disappears with a flush and a gurgle. "He's gone," sobs Plungo, staring disconsolately into the bowl. "Down the drain...."

Deep inside the earth, however, Pete finds himself launched on a strange, terrifying journey. Squeezed and stretched like putty, he is propelled through a tortuous maze of sewer pipes which grow tighter and tighter until they come to resemble an intestinal tract, too narrow to accommodate the pulpy plumber. Unable to budge, Pete begins to panic as the pressure builds up behind him. Finally, covered from head to toe with excrement, he explodes into a mysterious chamber inhabited by a bunch of "shitheads"—men like himself who have tried to commit suicide by taking "a one-way trip down the bathroom bowl." None of these sorry creatures knows exactly where he's landed: "I think it's a filter—a kind of depository built into the sewage system," speculates one. "No, no, you got it all wrong!" another replie

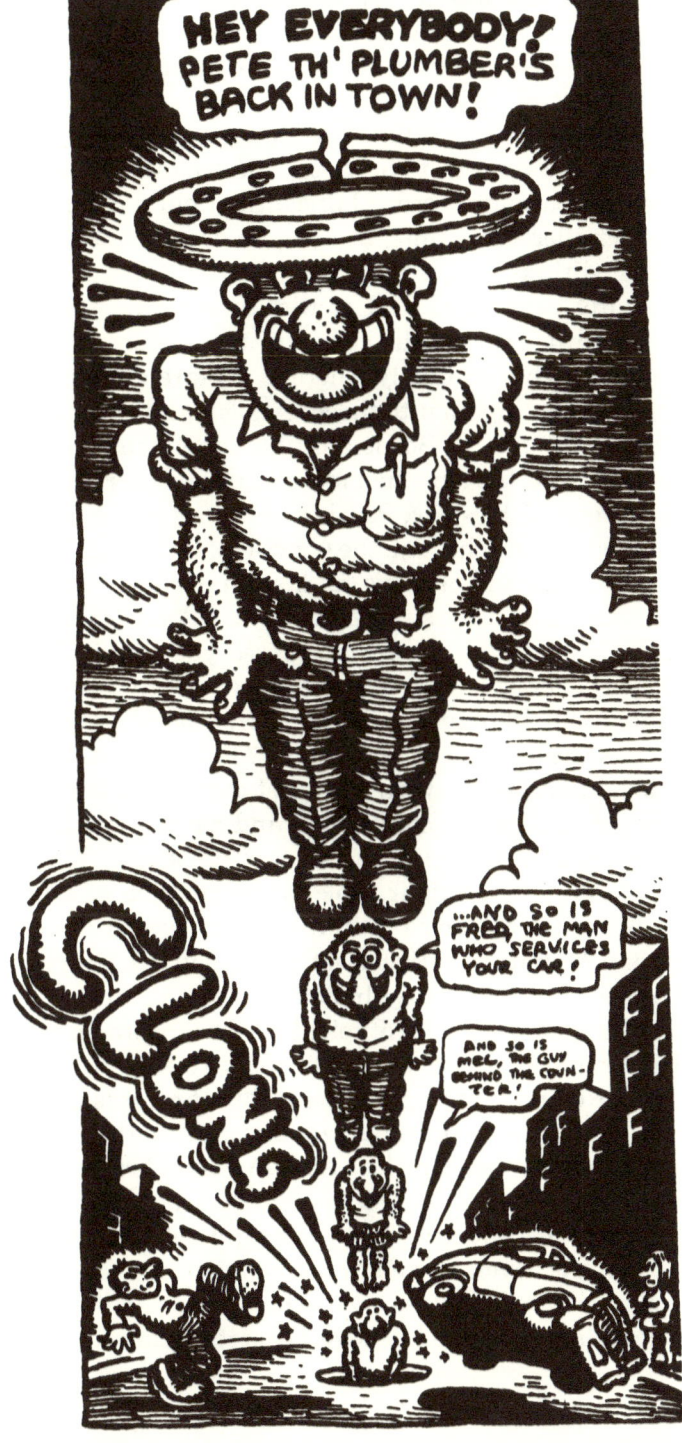

Reprinted with permission from R. Crumb for panels from "Pete the Plumber."

"It's some sort of waiting room for lost souls!" "Feh!" says a third, disgustedly. "You talk like the turds you are! I think what it is is we've all died and gone to Hell, that's what!"

Regretful now of their suicidal acts, Pete and the others decide to escape by taking the plunge down the mysterious black hole in the center of the floor. Once again, Pete finds himself shooting through a crazy labyrinth of pipes which grow smaller and smaller. This time, though, he doesn't get stuck, for as the pipes shrink into a network of capillaries, he feels himself "turning into jelly" and continues whirling through the tiny tubes until, nearing the center of the system, he dissolves in a flash of light. Suddenly, there is a blare of trumpets and Pete comes rocketing up into the streets, a manhole cover on his head like a halo (fig. 1). Borne aloft by angel wings, he and his pals dance across the sky, then march to loud cheers through the city. At the end of the story, Pete is a new man, reinvigorated and self-assured. Flying through the window of his house, he embraces his startled wife and plants a fat kiss on her lips. "Mmm, so good to see you again, my sweet!" he says. "There'll be some changes made 'round here, I can guarantee you that!" The final panel shows Pete striding triumphantly off to work, his faithful companion Plungo at his side. "Hey boss!" says Plungo. "It's great to be back on th' job! Isn't it? Huh?" "Yes, Plungo!" replies the plumber, who—with his chest thrust out, his head erect, his face radiant with confidence and vigor—looks twenty years younger than he did at the start of his story. "It is at that!"[1]

This funny, vulgar fable is the creation of an artist whose work we are already familiar with: the underground cartoonist Robert Crumb. A caricaturist of our culture, Crumb is also, as I have tried to show, a mythopoeic artist, and the world he portrays is inhabited by both protypical Americans and primordial gods. His vision, that is to say, is turned two ways, inward as well as outward, and if his comics are brilliant records of contemporary society, they also reflect a very different world: i.e., the collective unconscious, the "timeless and universal" realm of myth.[2] Like the other Crumb "comix" we have examined in this book—"Whiteman" and "Squirrely the Squirrel"—"Pete the Plumber" is, on one level, a humorous commentary on the life of the American middle-class. But what gives this story its "strange compelling power,"[3] I believe, is not its social satire but its mythic symbolism—for Pete's experience corresponds in every respect to that archetypal adventure story known variously as the night sea journey, the whale-dragon myth, the monomyth and the hero's quest.

The standard work on the subject of the quest archetype is Joseph Campbell's *Hero With a Thousand Faces,* which defines the features of the "universal mythological formula"[4] Campbell calls the monomyth. This "one, shape-shifting yet marvelously constant story," which, as Campbell demonstrates, underlies the myths and folktales of the world, is "a magnification of the formula represented in the rites of passage: *separation-initiation-return"* (30). Roused from the fixed routines of his life by some extraordinary event, the hero departs from the workaday world, crosses a threshold, and descends into the kingdom of darkness. There, he passes through a series of initiatory ordeals, achieves the boon he has been searching for, and returns, transfigured, to the daylight. While this boon, reward, or treasure, may assume an almost limitless variety of forms, "intrinsically," writes Campbell, "it is an expansion of consciousness and therewith of being" (246). Thus, as Campbell argues—and as Jung and other analytical psychologists confirm—the archetypal image of the hero's quest is a symbol for the process of self-realization or individuation. As Campbell explains,

It is the business of mythology proper, and of the fairy tale, to reveal the specific dangers and techniques of the dark interior way....Hence the incidents are fantastic and "unreal": they represent psychological, not physical, triumphs. Even when the legend is of an actual historical personage, the deeds of victory are rendered, not in lifelike, but in dreamlike figurations; for the point is not that such-and-such was done on earth; the point is that, before such-and-such could be done on earth, this other, more important, primary thing had to be brought to pass within the labyrinth that we all know and visit in our dreams. The passage of the mythological hero may be overground, incidentally; fundamentally it is inward—into depths where obscure resistances are overcome, and long lost, forgotten powers are revivified, to be made available for the transfiguration of the world (29).

The precise correspondence between the story of Pete and the primordial image of the hero's quest or night sea journey suggests that, in regard to Crumb's comic, we are dealing with a genuine archetypal revival: i.e., the spontaneous emergence of a mythic symbol from the depths of the collective unconscious. Like so many primitive myths and fairy tales, "Pete the Plumber" is set in a kind of wasteland: the world Crumb's character inhabits is blighted by financial and domestic woes. Typically, the hero's quest begins with some sort of summons or "call to adventure." Here, the herald or "announcer of the adventure" (53) is the plumber's friend, Plungo, who sets Pete's quest in motion when he comes running in to announce the evening headlines. Pete then descends in death by taking a suicidal plunge down the toilet bowl and enters a hellish underworld. After undergoing a severe trial, a painful and traumatic initiatory ordeal, he is rewarded with the boon of spiritual illumination or enlightenment, represented by his dissolution into a burst of blinding light when he reaches the center of the maze (fig. 2).

That Pete's trip through the labyrinth is indeed meant to symbolize a psychological voyage, an inner journey leading toward "an expansion of consciousness," is made clear in an interesting way by Crumb himself. "Pete the Plumber" is the lead story in an underground comic book entitled *Your Hytone Comix* and is followed immediately in this magazine by something called the "Puzzle Page"—Crumb's parody of one of those labyrinth-games which are generally found in children's publications and which ask the reader to trace the path of a complicated maze with a pencil. Crumb's version of this game takes the form of a cut-away view of a man's head, the inside of which is filled with the same sort of serpentine maze, leading directly to a patch of glowing light at its center, which we find in "Pete the Plumber." The instructions for this puzzle read: "Help this brilliant young fellow to find spiritual enlightenment by following the twisted path which leads to the void at the center of his brain."[5]

That a comic book can correspond with such precision to the "standard path of the mythological adventure of the hero" (30) should come as no surprise, since we have already seen, in the story of the origin of Captain Marvel, an example of a comic book which exactly conforms to the pattern of the monomyth. My intention in the present chapter is to take an even closer look at the monomyth as it appears in the popular arts. To do this, I propose to analyze in detail a single work: the film version of Jules Verne's *Journey to the Center of the Earth*. I've picked this

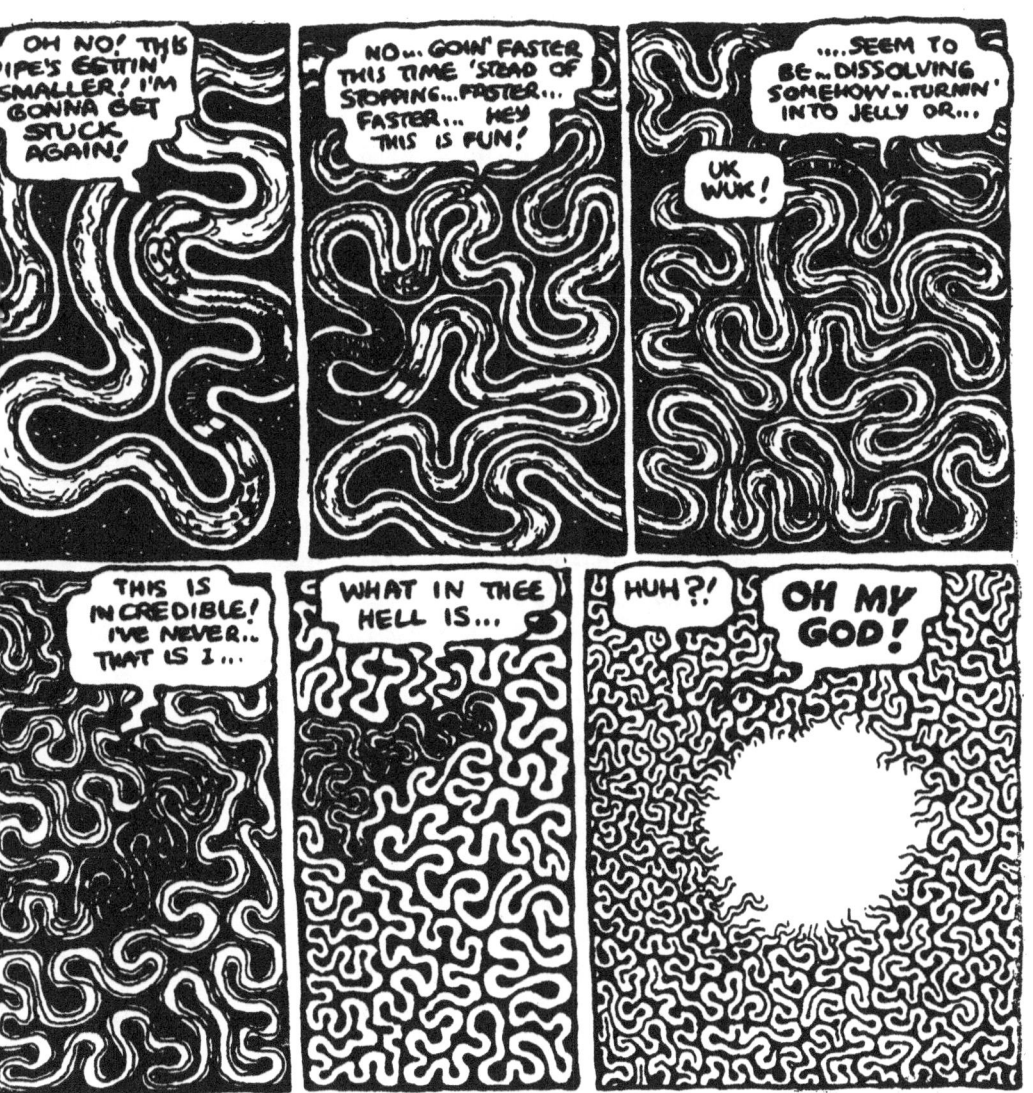

Reprinted with permission from R. Crumb for panels from "Pete the Plumber."

particular movie because it is a prototypical piece of American popular culture—a slick, commercially successful product of the Hollywood dream factory—with surprisingly rich archetypal content. As such, it is representative of the kind of material not generally included in studies of the hero's quest. Campbell, for instance, does not deal at all with movies, comic books, science fiction novels, or any other form of mass entertainment in his study. Had he done so, he would have been obliged to call the book *Hero With 2000 Faces;* for, as I hope to show, the quest archetype is as central to popular culture as it is to primitive myths and fairy tales.

2

The opening scenes of *Journey to the Center of the Earth* are set in a storybook version of Victorian Edinburgh—the sort of tidy, conventional world quest stories often begin in. This is the realm associated with consciousness and control; a safe structured, sunlit world—which, however, in its very orderliness and familiarity may come to seem (as it does, for example, to Ed Gentry, the protagonist of Dickey's *Deliverance*) sterile and constraining: a kind of wasteland.

The hero of the movie is Professor Oliver Lindenbrook (played by James Mason). Lindenbrook has just been knighted, and we first see him as he strolls along the streets, receiving the congratulations of his neighbors. Purchasing his morning paper, he becomes so engrossed in reading it that he walks, face buried in its pages, through the middle of a noisy parade of kilt-wearing, bagpipe-blowing Scotsmen. We are meant to recognize Lindenbrook as the prototypical pedant—the absent-minded professor—whose intellect has become so overdeveloped that he tends to be oblivious of the world outside. The Edinburgh portrayed at the start of the movie is a place dominated by "male intellectual consciousness" (in Erich Neumann's words) or "father thinking" (in Robert Bly's). It is a strictly patriarchal world, a world of bright daylight and masculine pursuits, where the qualities most valued are clear, linear thinking, competition and performance.

Walking into his lecture hall, Lindenbrook, the revered father figure, is greeted by the cheers of his all-male students, and after receiving their congratulatory gift—an atrocious inkstand made of ram's horns, the kind of aggressively masculine present one would expect from a group of bluff, well-meaning boys—he repays them with fatherly kindness, dismissing them early from school: "Now, off to the playing fields with you!" An embodiment of patriarchal Logos, the bachelor Lindenbrook has little use for women or for feminine values—emotion, intuition—in general. His paternalistic, condescending treatment of women—of his housekeeper and of his niece Jenny—barely conceals his contempt. The anti-feminine feelings expressed by the protagonist are very much those of a pre-adolescent male who views all women as meddling mother-figures, an attitude we should not be surprised to find in what is primarily a boy's adventure movie. But the fact that the film has deep appeal for adults as well as for children suggests that the hero's misogyny reflects a widespread cultural attitude. Lindenbrook is representative of Western hyperrational man, completely cut off, to the detriment of his spiritual well-being, from the sphere of the Feminine. To redeem his life from its unhealthy, one-sided orientation, "its too exclusive reliance on intellect, reasoning, and consciously directed will power,"[6] he will have to integrate this sphere into his conscious personality by undertaking the inner quest for self-realization.

Characteristically, Lindenbrook's quest is set in motion by a "call to adventure." The mythological call or summons may assume a variety of forms. Sometimes, a "herald" will arrive on the scene, begging the hero's assistance in, or challenging him to undertake, a perilous enterprise. We see this motif in works ranging from *The Faerie Queene*—in which the Red Crosse Knight is launched on his great adventure when Una appears at Queen Gloriana's court, pleading for a champion who will free her parents' kingdom from the dragon that is ravaging the land—to the cowboy film *The Magnificent Seven,* in which the aid of a gallant band of gunslingers is sought by some poor Mexican farmers, whose village, like Una's homeland, is being terrorized by an evil power (though in this case it is a gang of bandits instead of a dragon).

At other times, the call may take the form of a feeling *within* the hero, a craving for the new and exciting. The plot of *Deliverance* begins with just such a call—the narrator's strong, if ill-defined, urge for change, for transformation—as does the action of *Moby-Dick,* in which Ishmael is impelled to set forth on his sea-quest by his "hypos." Finally, the hero may be summoned to adventure by an unusual object or incident—something which unexpectedly disrupts his day-to-day routines. In the phenomenally successful *Star Wars,* for example, Luke Skywalker's intergalactic exploits start with the sudden appearance at his uncle's "moisture farm" of a strange little robot programmed to transmit a cryptic message. The marvelous adventures of Dorothy, the young heroine of L. Frank Baum's *The Wonderful Wizard of Oz,* begin when an extraordinary cyclone transports the girl from the "great, gray" wasteland of the Kansas prairie to a lush, enchanted land. And the accidental discovery of a simple, seemingly innocuous gold ring leads to the momentous events chronicled in Tolkien's famous quest-narrative, *The Lord of the Rings.*

This last form of the call is the kind we find in *Journey to the Center of the Earth,* for Lindenbrook's quest commences with the intrusion of a mysterious, intriguing object into his safe, settled, orderly life. This object is an unusually heavy piece of "Icelandic lava" which one of his students, Alec McKuen (played by Pat Boone) has acquired with the money left over after the purchase of the inkstand. That this simple piece of rock does indeed function as a mythological herald, issuing a call to heroic adventure, is made very clear in the movie. "I saw it in the window of an antique shop," says Alec, explaining how he came to purchase the chunk of lava. "It seemed to whisper to me, 'Buy me for Professor Lindenbrook'."

Puzzled by the exceptional weight of the lava, Lindenbrook retreats that evening to his basement lab, where, with the help of his assistant, Mr. Paisley, he runs the rock through a series of tests, completely forgetting about the dinner party taking place in his honor. When his pretty niece Jenny arrives to ask how long he will be busy with his experiments, he replies in his usual misogynous manner: "A typically female question," he snorts. At that moment, Mr. Paisley, who has been paying more attention to the exchange between Lindenbrook and Jenny than to the delicate task he has been assigned, accidentally sets off an explosion. When the smoke clears, Lindenbrook, thrown to the floor, discovers that the force of the blast has completely shattered the lava, revealing a peculiar metal object which was embedded within. "Mr. Paisley," cries Lindenbrook, as he eagerly examines this object, "by your slip you have rendered an inestimable service to science!"

This accident is the first of several fortuitous events which occur in the film, each of which ends by "rendering an inestimable service" to the hero. Though they are attributed to specific causes, the very consistency with which these accidents issue in happy results suggests that there is something providential about them. In fact, these unforeseen occurrences, which lend support to the hero at critical points on his quest, are examples of the common mythological motif that Campbell calls *supernatural aid.* Wherever this motif appears, in myths, movies, fairy tales or science fiction, its symbolic meaning is always the same: it tells us that logic has its limitations and can carry us only so far, and that—when we are faced with a problem we cannot think our way clear of, when our rational minds have reached a dead end—there are other, unconscious powers which can help and sustain us, if we will only learn to trust in them, to leave ourselves open to their promptings. Like so many heroes of the quest, Lindenbrook comes to heed and respect the guidance of these powers, which send up their messages from some dark, deep place far below the bright, rational world he is master of.

The strange black object found inside the volcanic lava is the bearer of one such message from the subterranean realm. Inspecting it, Lindenbrook discovers that it is an explorer's plumb bob, covered with foreign words written, apparently, in blood. The words prove to be those of the great sixteenth century scientist Arne Saknussem, who disappeared centuries before, "never to be heard from until tonight!" Saknussem's communication, written in the shaky hand of a dying man, provides directions for reaching the center of the earth. Lindenbrook is, of course, extremely excited by this discovery, never for a moment doubting its authenticity. Like the fairy tale hero who accepts without question the guidance of various magical powers, Lindenbrook has implicit faith in the miraculous forces which have placed Saknussem's plumb bob in his hands. As we shall see, Saknussem himself is present throughout the movie, in spirit if not in person, playing a role analogous to that of the mythic Wise Old Man or the fairy godmother: the guardian angel who comes to the hero's aid at moments of uncertainty and crisis.

Sir Oliver hastens to send news of his discovery to a renowned colleague, Professor Goetaborg of Stockholm. Receiving no reply, Lindenbrook becomes suspicious, and his fears are confirmed when he learns that Goetaborg has abruptly set out for Iceland. Lindenbrook, accompanied by Alec, soon follows, only to find when he arrives in Reykjavik that Goetaborg has bought up all the equipment—ropes, lanterns, climbing boots, and other supplies—necessary for the underground expedition. Moreover, Goetaborg's villainy does not end with his appropriation of Lindenborg's find, for, upon learning that his rival has landed in Iceland, he arranges to have Sir Oliver and Alec kidnapped and imprisoned in a remote, eiderdown storehouse. The shifty-eyed, weasel-faced Goetaborg is a shadow figure of the noble Lindenbrook, a sinister threshold guardian who stands between the hero and his goal and who must be defeated before Lindenbrook can pass onto the road of adventure.

The hero and his young sidekick are freed from their prison by a genial blond giant named Hans, who, despite the fact that he speaks no English and can therefore barely communicate with the Scotsmen, immediately becomes Lindenbrook's devoted servant. That "the big Icelander" (as Hans is called in the film) should offer a total stranger such instantaneous and unquestioning allegiance makes no logical sense; but it makes a good deal of mythological sense, for if Goetaborg is Sir Oliver's negative shadow figure—a symbol of the extreme ambitiousness and greed for glory which the hero has never faced up to in himself—the Herculean Hans is Lindenbrook's *positive* shadow, a symbol of the physical, instinctual side of the hyperintellectual scientist. Thus, Lindenbrook and Hans are intimately connected, as Ishmael is to Queequeg or the Lone Ranger to Tonto. Hans' role as an embodiment of constructive instinct is made clear not only by his own physical attributes—primarily the superhuman strength which he puts at Lindenbrook's disposal—but also by his loving attachment to a pet duck named Gertrude, who, as I indicated in an earlier chapter, functions in the film as an archetypal helpful animal.

Having been rescued by Hans, Lindenbrook and Alec hurry back to their hotel—the same one Herr Goetaborg is staying at—

intent on confronting their kidnapper. Entering his rooms, they are astonished to discover their rival's dead body, laid out beneath a sheet. Goetaborg, it turns out, has been poisoned by an even greater villain: the fiendish Count Saknussem, a descendant of the famous sixteenth-century scientist. We first see Saknussem on a pitch black night as he stands on the crest of a volcano, his bloated lizard's face luridly illuminated by the light of the flaring torch that he carries. Compared to Saknussem, Goetaborg was a minor criminal, for whereas the renegade professor represented the personal shadow—the repressed, detested part of the hero's personality—Saknussem is a collective shadow symbol, an embodiment of the dark, demonic side of human nature in general.

He is, in short, the devil, and his satanic character is made abundantly clear in the movie by his repeated insistence that he is the lord of the underworld. "I am the owner of this domain!" he declares at one point later on in the movie, referring to the subterranean realm, and his tone is so imperious that Lindenbrook and the others begin speaking of him, with heavy sarcasm, as "his highness" and "his majesty." But such epithets, though meant ironically, have more truth in them than the hero and his companions know, for the count is indeed "his majesty"—His Satanic Majesty—the archetypal adversary whose existence within every human psyche must be faced up to and acknowledged if self-realization is to proceed. As the analytical psychologist Liliane Frey-Rohn points out, "studies of the individuation process corroborate the fact that *there can be no self-realization without the experience of evil*":

...at a certain moment in life, not only the personally repressed and inferior, but also the immoral, the pathological, and even the senseless, acquire the importance of a *conditio sine qua non* for psychic renewal. That evil can point the way to psychic totality appears astonishing from the standpoint of traditional morality. But this is possible because evil has preserved the original connection with the archetypes and the age-old paths of nature; it has access to the lost depths of the soul, to the vast background of human culture....Under favorable circumstances, this enables the adversary to act as a bridge which reunites man with the source of life. The potentially positive function of evil is therefore to bring man back to his source and, simultaneously, to his unrealized higher meanings. Thus evil may open the way for spiritual renewal and relationship to the self.[7]

Lindenbrook, however, will not confront the archetypal

shadow until he has descended into the dark, dangerous kingdom whose threshold he is now prepared to cross. With Goetaborg out of the way, only one obstacle remains: Goetaborg's attractive wife, Carla (played by Arlene Dahl), who, having arrived at the scene, has taken possession of her husband's property, including all the gear Lindenbrook needs for his journey. At first Carla refuses to relinquish the equipment, taking umbrage when Lindenbrook lays claim to it. But when—while reading through her dead husband's diary—she discovers evidence of Goetaborg's iniquity, she relents and offers the equipment to Lindenbrook, placing one condition, however, on the gift. She insists on accompanying the three men, Sir Oliver, Alec and Hans, on their expedition. The professor, with his fierce, anti-feminine prejudices, is outraged. "You can't come along!" he cries. "You're a woman!" But finally, having no choice if he is to accomplish his mission, he concedes. In order to achieve the "ultimate boon" of self-realization, Lindenbrook, like all heroes of the quest, must learn to establish a new and more balanced relationship not only with the shadow but also with the anima—with the feminine personality components he has always denigrated and denied a place to in his life.

On the following morning, the four explorers climb to the top of a volcano to begin their long descent, and here, at the very start of their journey, another miraculous event occurs. A single ray of the rising sun pierces through a narrow crack in nearby Mt. Scartaris and, like a celestial signpost, points directly to an otherwise invisible opening in the crater's side: the entrance to the path leading to the center of the earth. Though a rational explanation is given for this occurrence (Arne Saknussem's message has indicated that, on a particular day of the year, Scartaris would show the way), the obvious impossibility of the phenomenon (how could Saknussem have known that this single sunbeam would guide him straight to his goal?) marks it as yet another example of supernatural aid, what Joseph Campbell calls "the benign, protecting power of destiny" (71).

Arriving at the ledge revealed by Scartaris, Lindenbrook is momentarily baffled, unable to find the opening in the rock. It is at this point that Hans' pet duck Gertrude, the mascot of the expedition, wanders away and waddles through a concealed crevice, revealing the entrance to the underworld. As I indicated in my earlier discussion of the helpful animal, Sir Oliver's readiness to let Gertrude lead the way is the sign of the hero's increasing reliance on, and respect for, animal instinct—a mark of his movement toward psychic totality.

Once the four adventurers have squeezed through the crack, they find themselves in a shadowy and mysterious realm. At this point, the hero and his companions have left the bright, familiar world behind and crossed the threshold into the "kingdom of the dark" (245)—a passage which is represented in many different ways in the myths, folktales and symbolic stories of the world. The quest of the mythic hero may lead him from the comforts of hearth and home to the depths of a cave, the gloom of an enchanted forest, the bottom of an ocean or the belly of a dragon. Sometimes, the hero literally descends into Hades, while at other times, the hell he enters is purely metaphoric: the fictional private eye, for instance, generally sets out from the safety of his office or apartment to pursue his investigations in a dark, criminal underworld. Jungians call this mythological descent the night sea journey or the *nekyia* (a term derived from the eleventh book of the *Odyssey*, in which the hero journeys down into the land of the dead).

Whatever form this motif takes, it always stands for the psychological descent into the darkness of the unconscious, into the depths of our own unexplored interiors—a process which invariably entails a kind of initiatory death, the casting off of our old personalities, followed, ideally, by our "inner transformation and rebirth into another being," the reconstitution of a new, more integrated Self.[8] To undergo such a process, however, requires a great deal of courage, since self-discovery—the confrontation with repressed psychic contents—is a painful, even perilous, enterprise. "Explore thyself," says Thoreau in *Walden*. "Herein are demanded the eye and the nerve."[9] The unconscious teems with dangerous powers which can overwhelm and even disintegrate the ego. Thus, Campbell describes the mythic hero's path as "the road of trials," for it is filled with terrifying ordeals which threaten the hero with annihilation.

Throughout *Journey to the Center of the Earth*, Lindenbrook, Alec, Hans and Carla face numerous dangers. Early on in their journey, they are almost crushed when a colossal boulder, dislodged from its precarious perch high above them, comes hurtling down the narrow corridor they are passing through. Later, Alec becomes separated from the rest of the group and gets lost in the labyrinthine pathways of the underworld. Various calamities befall him: a narrow stone bridge he tries to cross collapses under his feet, nearly hurling him into a bottomless pit. Soon after, as he stumbles through a desert of salt, the ground dissolves beneath his feet and, like sand in an hourglass, he is sucked down through a narrow opening and plunged into a cavern hundreds of feet below.

Lindenbrook, meanwhile, having discovered a dazzling, crystalline garden in an underground chamber, resolves to take a sample of the precious stone. Removing a small chunk with hammer and chisel, he turns away. Behind his back, however, the rock springs a leak; a moment later, the trickle turns into a torrent and, within seconds, the chamber is flooded and the small band of explorers nearly drowned as the waters rise inexorably to the ceiling. Other near-disasters occur: at one point, many months into the descent, the travellers' electric lamps give out, and they are faced with the prospect of being plunged into impenetrable darkness. At another point, Carla comes close to being devoured by a giant carnivorous lizard; she is rescued in the nick of time by Hans, who slays the prehistoric monster with a pikestaff. And, toward the end of their journey, the travellers are very nearly drowned in a giant whirlpool as they make their way across a great subterranean sea.

All of these ordeals symbolize the perils of the descent into the dream world of the unconscious, where the ego may easily be disoriented, disintegrated, devoured or drowned. Significantly— despite the scientific aura which surrounds the action of the film—the tests and ordeals which the explorers undergo are the archetypal hero's trials common to myth and folklore. The flimsy span of stone which Alec attempts to cross, for instance, is a version of the well-known motif of the "sword bridge," an archetypal ordeal in which the hero "must cross an abyss by means of a bridge as narrow as the edge of a knife."[10]

The pretty crystal rock which unleashes a lethal flood when Lindenbrook removes a small piece of it is analogous to a motif found in "Beauty and the Beast" and other fairy tales, in which a character, a traveller in a strange place, comes upon an alluring, seemingly harmless object and takes possession of it, only to find that he has thereby released a terrifyingly destructive power. This motif symbolizes the dangers of tampering with the alien forces of the unconscious—forces which, as Campbell reminds us, are both "fiendishly fascinating" and extremely dangerous (8). And in the scene in which Hans saves Carla from the dinosaur, we see an updated image of the knight in shining armor rescuing the captive damsel from the clutches of the fire-breathing dragon.

Lindenbrook and his friends, however, survive all these perils. Two things protect them on their hazardous voyage. First, there is the supernatural aid they receive from various sources. Like the archetypal quest hero described by Campbell, Sir Oliver enters a frightening underground realm, only to find "that there is a benign power everywhere supporting him in his superhuman passage" (97). The explorers escape the boulder, for instance, by leaping from a ledge and throwing themselves face down on the ground beneath it. The great stone goes hurtling over their heads and, with a tremendous crash, shatters against the opposite wall. When the dust clears, Lindenbrook, lying flat on his stomach, sees before him three distinctive grooves cut deep into the rock floor—an unmistakable trail marker made by the pioneering Arne Saknussem. Thus, another "accident"—very similar to the one which happened earlier in the laboratory—has led the hero to a sign from the legendary explorer who, once again, functions as Lindenbrook's guardian angel, offering guidance from beyond the grave.

Unbeknownst to Sir Oliver and his friends, however, Saknussem's evil descendant has been shadowing them throughout their journey, and at one point he conceals the original trail markings and substitutes phony ones which almost lead the four explorers to their doom. Lindenbrook is baffled by the misleading sign until Gertrude the duck comes to his aid once more. With her instinctive knowledge of the true path, she is able to steer Lindenbrook and the others to the genuine marks and thus serves to warn them of the danger close at hand. Supernatural aid also manifests itself when the electric lamps carried by Sir Oliver's party run down and the terrifying darkness of the underworld closes around the adventurers. At that very moment, the walls of the chamber they are in begin to glow with a glorious light. Once again, a scientific explanation is given for the phenomenon—the walls, we are told, are covered with "a form of algae with the property of luminescence"—but it is clear that this remarkable light is as magical as that contained in the small crystal phial bestowed by the Elf-queen Galadriel on Frodo the hobbit in Tolkien's *The Fellowship of the Ring:* a gift to guide the ring-bearer "in the dark, when all other lights go out."[11]

But there is something else besides the supernatural help they receive which accounts for the survival of Lindenbrook's party, and that is the cooperation and interdependence of its members. For what this small group of four symbolizes is that invincible psychic totality which Jung calls the *quaternity* and which is composed of "the four functions of consciousness"— thinking, feeling, sensation and intuition—operating in balance and harmony. According to analytical psychology, these four psychic functions are the "means by which consciousness obtains its orientation to experience. *Sensation* (i.e., sense perception) tells you that something exists; *thinking* tells you what it is; *feeling* tells you whether it is agreeable or not; and *intuition* tells you whence it comes and where it is going."[12] In his introduction to *The Portable Jung,* Joseph Campbell provides a neat summary of this concept[13] and explains that "Jung's concept is that the aim of one's life, psychologically speaking, should be not to suppress or repress, but to come to know one's other side, and so both to enjoy and to control the whole range of one's capacities; i.e., in the full sense, to 'know oneself.' "[14] This state of self-knowledge, as we have seen, is achieved through the process of individuation. The union of psychic opposites which results from this process is represented by the ancient symbol of the quaternity, an archetypal image of wholeness and harmony:

Sensation

Feeling ———— Thinking

Intuition

As the symbol of psychic integration, the quaternity is frequently found in popular art, since a central theme of such art, as I have been arguing, is the way of individuation. In her quest to find the wonderful Wizard of Oz, for example, Dorothy encounters, and immediately forms a deep and abiding attachment to, three remarkable figures: an extremely shrewd Scarecrow who believes he has no brains, a sentimental Tin Woodman who thinks he is heartless, and a courageous Cowardly Lion. These three characters, together with Dorothy, form a single, indivisible unit—a quarternity—in which the Scarecrow stands for thinking, the Tin Woodman for feeling, the Lion for sensation (a category often symbolized by very physical, earthy, or even animalistic beings) and Dorothy for intuition (traditionally, though not exclusively, associated with the feminine).

The four main characters of the popular television program *Star Trek* likewise form a quarternity. Scotty, the chief engineer of the *Enterprise,* who is always toiling in the bowels of the ship, keeping the machinery in working order, is—like Hawthorne's character Aminadab (in "The Birthmark") or the dwarfish Igor of the Frankenstein films—an embodiment of "man's physical nature"[15] and thus a symbol of sensation. The hyperrational science officer, Mr. Spock, personifies thinking, while the ship's excitable, fiery physician, "Bones" McCoy, stands for feeling. And Captain Kirk, who, in reaching his decisions, relies as much on his hunches as on his head and heart (logic and emotion) is representative of intuition. Similarly, the early episodes of another successful television series, *Bonanza,* feature four main characters—the all-male members of the Cartwright family— who also constitute a quaternity. Sensation is symbolized by the Herculean brother, Hoss; intuition by the sensitive, poetic Adam; feeling by the hot-blooded Little Joe; and thinking by their father Ben, the head of the clan.

On certain rare occasions, the quaternity may even manifest itself in life, shaping the destinies of actual people.[16] That is, four individuals, each representing one of the four different functions, will come together to form a powerful unit, a whole that is somehow greater than the sum of its parts. This was the case, I believe, with the four Beatles—John Lennon, Paul McCartney, George Harrison and Ringo Starr—who often claimed that they were four separate parts of a single personality. The literate, sardonic Lennon stood for thinking; Harrison—deeply immersed in Eastern mysticism—for intuition; the romantic, androgynously pretty McCartney, for feeling; and the clownish Ringo, with his puppy-dog charm, for sensation. Together these four musicians constituted an astonishingly creative and dynamic entity; separated from one another, however, they seem to have lost most of their artistic power.[17]

In *Journey to the Center of the Earth,* the members of the Lindenbrook expedition form an archetypal quaternity of sensation (Hans, the embodiment of brute strength), feminine intuition (Carla), feeling (Alec, the young romantic, who is constantly sighing for his faraway sweetheart, Jenny) and thinking (the professor). Working together as a team, this foursome, symbolizing the integrated Self, succeeds in carrying out an apparently impossible mission. The message here is the same one that is unconsciously conveyed, as Bruno Bettelheim has shown, by so many fairy tales: that "after we have achieved an integrated personality, we can accomplish what seem like miracles."[18] Significantly, the worst calamity that occurs in the film is the separation of Alec from the other members of the group, an event which leads to several serious mishaps (including the wounding of Alec) and which symbolizes the vulnerability of the disunited psyche, in contrast to the soundness and strength of the integrated Self.

Of course, psychic wholeness is not attained overnight. The four explorers do not work in perfect harmony from the very beginning of their quest, primarily because of Lindenbrook's tendency to distrust and disparage the Feminine. At one point, for example, near the start of the journey, as the travellers turn in for the night, Carla sits up with a start, certain that she has heard a sound over their heads. In fact, she has: Count Saknussem and his henchmen are lurking in the rocks above the explorers' camp. Lindenbrook, however, dismisses Carla's warning with a snide, sarcastic comment about "female intuition." It is not until their quest is nearly over that the hero is able to fully accept and establish an intimate connection with his anima-figure, thereby attaining the "treasure hard to attain"—the "ultimate boon" of psychic totality.

Before this happens, however, Lindenbrook must confront and come to terms with another archetypal figure: the collective shadow. This takes place when Alec—while wandering at a loss through the tortuous recesses of the underworld—suddenly comes upon the count, whose servant has died from fear and exhaustion. Saknussem, intending to make Alec his slave, holds a gun on the boy and commands him to pick up the fallen gear. When Alec refuses and turns to walk away, Saknussem shoots him in the arm. The gunfire brings Lindenbrook, Carla and Hans—who have been desperately searching for their lost companion—running. At last, the hero stands face to face with the personification of absolute evil. By a clever trick, Lindenbrook manages to seize the gun from Count Saknussem. Though the four travellers agree that the count deserves to die, none of them is willing to act as executioner. As a result, they decide to bring Saknussem along.

In psychological terms, this episode symbolizes that stage of the individuation process in which the ego finally encounters the archetypal shadow, the darkest portion of the human soul. Such evil is, ultimately, incorrigible; unlike the *personal* shadow—which consists of repressed psychic contents that can be raised to consciousness and given a measure of expression in one's life—the collective shadow cannot be assimilated or humanized. It can only be confronted and acknowledged as a living reality. Though Saknussem is compelled to accompany Lindenbrook's party, he is never integrated into it. He remains aloof, dedicated not, like the other explorers, to the general good of mankind, but strictly to himself. He corresponds exactly to the figure Campbell describes as the "tyrant-monster" of world mythology—"the monster avid for the greedy rights of 'my and mine' " (15). While Lindenbrook and the others enjoy a moment of happiness in a magical forest of giant mushrooms, for instance, Saknussem sneaks off and discovers a vast subterranean ocean, which he immediately names the Saknussem Sea.

It is while crossing this sea on a raft made from the trunks of the giant mushrooms that the hero reaches the goal he has been questing for. As the travellers sail along, all the metal objects in their possession—knives, rings, pens, compasses, even the gold in their teeth—suddenly fly off into the air. This startling phenomenon, Lindenbrook instantly realizes, is caused by the convergence of opposing magnetic forces, signifying that his expedition has finally reached the exact center of the earth. At this sacred spot, however—the *axis mundi,* the navel of the world—the energies of the universe are far too powerful to be tolerated by any man. The travellers are caught in a terrifying vortex and, stripped of everything but the clothes on their backs, cast up on a distant shore.

At this point—the point Campbell calls "the nadir of the mythological round" (246) Lindenbrook and Carla at last draw close, tacitly admitting their mutual love and falling asleep side by side on the sand. While they rest, Saknussem—who never sleeps, as he has informed Sir Oliver—kills and devours Gertrude the duck. In the eyes of the movie's young viewers, this act is undoubtedly the ultimate atrocity, proving once and for all that the evil which Saknussem personifies is an inescapable, ineradicable fact. When Hans awakens and discovers what has happened, he tries to strangle the count but is restrained by Sir Oliver and Alec. "You ingrate," cries Saknussem, as he leans, gasping, against a large rock. "What would you do without me? Only I can show you the way out of this realm of mine!" At that moment, the boulder he is resting against rolls loose, setting off a small avalanche with Saknussem in its midst, and the enemy plunges to his death. The supernatural powers which have guided and protected the hero throughout his quest are still at work: Saknussem's death is clearly an act of divine retribution. Moreover, like every other providential event that has occurred in the movie, this one leads the hero to an important discovery. The rockslide which has killed the count has also opened a break in the wall, revealing an astonishing sight: the lost city of Atlantis!

The hero has now reached the last stage of his mythological quest, the return. "If the powers have blessed the hero," writes Campbell, "he now sets forth under their protection" (246)—his ascent back into the daylight world is "supported by all the powers of his supernatural patron" (197). By an immense, still-intact bowl in which the city's sacrificial flame once burned, Lindenbrook discovers the remains of *his* "supernatural patron," Arne Saknussem. A guardian angel to the end, Saknussem lies with one arm thrown straight out, a bony finger pointing to an opening in a nearby wall. This hole turns out to be the entrance to a gigantic chimney leading directly to the surface.

Unfortunately, this route is blocked by an immovable boulder lodged part way up the shaft. Once again, however, Saknussem comes to the hero's rescue. His knapsack, perfectly preserved, is filled with dry, useable gunpowder. Lindenbrook, Alec and Hans pour some of the explosive around the boulder, fashion a fuse, ignite it and quickly take shelter, along with Carla, in the fireproof bowl. The blast sets off a volcanic reaction. Miraculously, the bowl is lifted up by the glowing red lava and borne directly into and straight up the chimney. Thus, the hero, blessed by the gods throughout his journey, returns to the surface, "carried along by the guiding divinities" (216).

Back in Edinburgh, Lindenbrook receives a tumultuous welcome. Though he has brought back no scientific proof of his discovery, he is greeted with applause and wild cheers, having returned transfigured, ready to "teach the lesson he has learned of life renewed" (20). The visible sign of his rebirth, of his achievement of a "bolder, cleaner, more spacious, and fully human life" (8), is his new love for Carla, to whom he proposes before the assembled multitude, there to do him honor. "The ultimate adventure," writes Campbell, "...is commonly represented as a mystical marriage...of the triumphant hero-soul with the Queen-Goddess of the World" (109). Embracing each other at last, Lindenbrook and Carla embody the mythic image of the syzygy, the archetypal conjunction of Father and Mother, Logos and Eros, Yin and Yang. Together, the pair symbolizes that wholeness which all the world celebrates as the perenniel source of "life-transmuting" power (193), and as the movie ends, the crowd gathered around the hero and his bride breaks into triumphant song.

Appendix

The Myth of the Eternal Child in Sixties America

Except ye become as little children, ye shall in no wise enter the kingdom of heaven.

Matthew 18:3

I came upon a child of god
He was walking along the road....
Joni Mitchell, "Woodstock"

1

I have spoken at several points in this study of Jung's theory of archetypal compensation. In this section, I wish to examine a specific and very striking instance of this phenomenon in order to demonstrate how the process of individuation may operate on a cultural scale. That is to say, I want to show how an archetypal image, a mythic symbol, can surface, at a particular historical moment, in the collective fantasies of a suffering society, forcing itself into the cultural consciousness in an apparently purposive attempt to restore psychic equilibrium.

Let me begin with a brief recapitulation of the theories this study has been based on. As we have seen, Jung believed that the unconscious consists of two separate, though interdependent, "strata," one personal, one *trans*personal. He called the latter the collective unconscious. This part of our minds does not develop out of our experiences as individuals; its contents are not acquired during our lives. Rather, it is inborn and universal: the same in everybody. Just as we all share a common human anatomy over and above the particular variations of our individual bodies, so, says Jung, we all share, at the deepest, most fundamental level of our beings, a common human psyche. Or, to put it another way, just as we all possess an anatomical structure that makes us recognizable as human beings (not as Tom or Harry or Judy or

140

Jane), so we all possess a basic psychic structure, a level of the mind, which is the source of our *typically human* perceptions, responses, ways of behaving in and relating to the world. This level of the psyche is the collective unconscious.

Now, just as the personal unconscious expresses itself, among other ways, in dreams, which are symbolic statements or stories which relate to and reveal truths about our personal lives and situations, so the collective unconscious expresses *itself* in dreams, but dreams whose symbols are common to us, and meaningful to us, as a species. Dreams which contain universal human truths. These collective dreams are what we mean by *myths*. Myths are the dreams of mankind, or, as Joseph Campbell puts it, "dream is the personalized myth, myth the depersonalized dream; both dream and myth are symbolic in the same general way of the dynamics of the psyche. But in the dream the forms are quirked by the particular troubles of the dreamer, whereas in myth the problems and solutions shown are directly valid for all mankind."[1] These mythic symbols which emerge from the collective unconscious Jung called archetypal images, and they appear in the imaginative products of the world, in all times and in all cultures—in religious mythologies, fairy tales, painting, classical literature, etc.

It was Jung's belief, moreover, that "the posture of the unconscious is compensatory to consciousness."[2] He conceived of the psyche as a self-regulating system, and held that when consciousness "so departs from the norms of the species that a pathological state of imbalance ensues, of neurosis or psychosis,"[3] the unconscious will respond by producing a corrective symbol in an effort to counterbalance the dangerous one-sidedness of the conscious attitude. In the case of a disturbed individual, this compensatory symbol will generally appear in his dreams. But as Jung shows, it is not only individuals who suffer from this kind of imbalance and whose lives require a compensatory adjustment but whole cultures, at different periods of time. And just as, in the case of the neurotic person, the healing symbol will appear in his dreams, so in the case of a disturbed society, the symbol will appear in *its* dreams. But what do we mean by the dreams of a culture? Where are they to be found? When we are talking about collective dreams we are really talking about myths. And in the modern world the myths or collective dreams of a culture are found predominantly in its popular art.

Not everyone, however, pays attention to his dreams; indeed, comparatively few people take them seriously. Thus, a critical question is raised in regard to this aspect of Jungian theory: namely, what happens if the conscious mind, as it so often does, ignores the message from the unconscious? Jung's answer is that archetypal symbols can manifest themselves not only in dream and myth but in human behavior, not only in art but in action. As he explains, symbols are "living psychic forces that demand to be taken seriously, and they have a strange way of making sure of their effect."[4] When an archetypal symbol emerges from the depths of the unconscious, it always brings with it what Jung calls a "compelling effect." It exerts a powerful influence on us. It can actually shape our lives to its ends, so that people in the grip of a symbol are impelled not only to portray it in art but to live it out in some way. They become *possessed* by the symbol. Such possession is the way the unconscious has of forcing us to recognize the symbol and to change our lives in accordance with the meaning it represents.

A good example of symbolic possession can be seen in the movie *Close Encounters of the Third Kind,* which portrays precisely this phenomenon: a group of people in the grip of a symbol. What happens to these people? First, they are moved by some inner necessity to embody or portray the symbol in some way: one character sculpts it, another paints it compulsively. But in larger terms, the symbol forces them into an awareness of, or confrontation with, something meaningful that has been completely missing from their lives: a sense of mystery, of the marvelous, the sublime. (The source of the symbol is shown to be outside the people, but this is just a case of the psychological mechanism of "projection.") It seems to me that the decision of the writer/director, Steven Spielberg, to set his movie in an absolutely flat, empty, Midwestern locale and to have the experience happen to utterly ordinary people leading utterly drab and mundane lives was perfect. He has either read Jung or intuited the same truth about compensatory symbols. Because the symbol which grips the imagination of his characters—and dramatically alters their lives—is compensatory to an existence which is completely devoid of any sense of the marvelous, of anything more sublime than a Budweiser beer commercial. The symbol which possesses them is the precise opposite of the mundane; it is otherworldly, celestial—a great, vaulting, magic mountain crowned with a halo of heavenly light. Essentially, it is a religious symbol which these characters are compelled to integrate into their heretofore spirit-less lives, or else run the risk of suffering a total psychic collapse.

So, to sum up, we see that, at certain periods, in societies which have been moving in a dangerously one-sided direction, in which certain values and attitudes are emphasized to the unhealthy exclusion of other important ones, a mythic symbol will arise which will possess the imagination of large numbers of people—dominate their dreams, even shape their destinies. And this symbol will be compensatory to the outlook of the culture at large, to its dominant values and beliefs and practices. It will represent an attempt to correct, or redirect the energies of, the culture.

2

In our own culture, such a symbol emerged, I believe, during the 1960s.

Interest in the sixties is running high these days. Scholarly studies on the subject have begun to appear, Beatlemania is back, and many people, particularly those too young to have participated themselves, seem endlessly fascinated by the landmark events of the time: Woodstock, the peace protests, the Summer of Love. It is possible, I suppose, to interpret all this interest as just the next logical phase in the nostalgia boom, the fifties having been milked dry by the media. But there is a significant difference between the ways in which the fifties and the sixties are perceived, for while the fifties have been transmuted into Happy Days, a prefabricated fairy tale,[5] the sixties are coming to seem more and more like a truly mythic age. Morris Dickstein, in his excellent study *Gates of Eden,* captures this sense of the sixties very well when he quotes two of the more common, current responses to the era: "Was it that long ago? did all that really happen?"[6]

The interesting question is: how do we account for the legendary air which this period has taken on in the minds of so many people? The answer, I believe, is that the sixties always *were* a mythic age, even while they were taking place, though few people could perceive this at the time. We are rarely aware of the myths we are living out, or living within, while we are in the midst of them. But now that we have some distance from the decade, its mythic quality is becoming more clear. This discussion, then, represents another attempt to make sense of the sixties—not their social or political or economic significance but their mythological importance. What was the principal myth of the sixties?

The symbol which dominated that decade—which gave it shape, direction, meaning—is the one which Jungians call the *puer aeternus:* the eternal child (known also as the eternal youth or immortal child).

Exactly what is the *puer aeternus?* The standard work on the subject, Marie-Louise von Franz's book *The Problem of the Puer Aeternus,* contains the following definition:

> *Puer aeternus* is the name of a god of antiquity. The words themselves come from Ovid's *Metamorphoses* and are there applied to the child-god in the Eleusinian mysteries. Ovid speaks of the child-god Iacchus, addressing him as *puer aeternus*....In later times, the child-god was identified with Dionysus and the god Eros. He is the divine youth who is born in the night....He is a god of vegetation and resurrection, the god of divine youth, corresponding to such oriental gods as Tammuz, Attis, and Adonis. The title *puer aeturnus* therefore means eternal youth....[7]

The term *puer aeternus,* then, applies first of all to certain mythological figures, primarily young male deities who die in their youths and are usually reborn. Frequently, they are vegetation gods, like Attis, Tammuz, or Adonis, who die or are slain and then are resurrected in the spring—so that they become, in effect, undying, immortal, eternally youthful. Sometimes, like Hyacinth and Narcissus, they are reborn or resurrected as flowers—i.e., they are flower-people, flower-children. Mythic figures who fall into the category of *puer aeternus* (besides the ones already mentioned) include Dionysus, Hippolytus, Bellerophon, Icarus, Hermes and Pan.[8]

All myths, all archetypal images, are metaphors or symbols of certain psychological traits (so that when we talk about being possessed by an archetype, we mean that, in such situations, our psychological lives become "mimetic to myths," imitate or recreate myths. Our behavioral patterns match or follow mythic patterns.)[9] The primary psychological trait associated with the eternal child is, obviously, a refusal to grow up—a desire to remain a child forever. This characteristic is closely connected to several others. First, there is the trait which might best be labelled *timelessness:* the urge to drop out of time and history and inhabit a paradise or Never Never Land free of the responsibilities and obligations of adulthood, to remain in a state of what Norman O. Brown calls "privileged irresponsibility."[10] Second, there is what von Franz describes as a terrible fear of being pinned down in the "real world," of being caught in a situation from which it may be impossible to slip out again. And this fear is inseparable from another typical *puer* trait described by von Franz: a difficulty with making a definite commitment to another person or to a personal relationship.

Another feature of *puer* psychology discussed by both von Franz and the Jungian analyst James Hillman is "ascensionism": a fascination with ascending, with heights and flying. Von Franz describes ascensionism as "a desire to get as high as possible, the symbolism being to get away from reality, from the earth, from ordinary life."[11] The *puer* types from classical mythology include Icarus, who flew too near the sun on his wings of wax and feathers, and Bellerophon, who tried to ride to the top of Mount Olympus on the back of the winged horse Pegasus.

There is an intense feeling or sympathy for nature associated with the *puer aeternus*. As I noted above, many *puer* figures are vegetation gods and are closely connected in their myths to Earth Mother goddesses: Attis and Cybele, Osiris and Isis, Tammuz and Ishtar.

Puer aeternus psychology is also distinguished by a tendency to divinize or demonize adults. Just as a child will perceive grown-ups, and especially his parents, as larger-than-life, supernatural beings—gods or demons—so there is a corresponding tendency among *puer* types to see adults in this exaggerated fashion.

The eternal child is further characterized by androgyny—an ambiguous sexuality or bisexuality which displays both masculine and feminine characteristics.

Finally, two last traits associated with the eternal child: holy innocence and tricksterism. By holy innocence, I mean an attitude of childlike innocence and simplicity in one's dealing with the world. The holy innocent is a person who goes against the conventional wisdom of the world. He (or she) does not operate by the usual standards of profit and practicality. Rather, he lives by other, higher laws. He doesn't care about "getting ahead" or "making it," which of course renders him totally unsuited to the "serious" business of the world. Instead of following the dictates of a society that puts a premium on material advancement and financial success, he spends his time in such "idle" pursuits as contemplation or communion with nature. As a result, he is regarded as a fool by those members of society who prize common sense and tough-mindedness (the "when-the-going-gets-tough-the tough-get-going" types, the hard-chargers). So the holy innocent is also sometimes known as the holy fool.

The meaning of tricksterism has already been examined at length in Chapter Three. As we saw there, the trickster represents a powerfully anarchic, anti-authoritarian impulse—a drive to revolt, to disrupt or overturn the existing order—and, especially in American folklore and popular culture, is commonly symbolized by a mischievous child, a bad boy.

When we look at American society in the sixties, at the counterculture during those years, we discover that it is characterized by precisely those traits which define the *puer aeternus* archetype. First of all, we find a group of people who identify themselves as children, and not just children but flower-children. The original flower-children, as we have seen, were the *pueri* of classical mythology, like Hyacinth and Narcissus. And this fact in itself suggests that what was taking place in the sixties was the revival of an ancient mythic idea—the recurrence of what Jung calls a "primordial image."

That a mythic revival of this sort occurred during the sixties becomes even more clear when we consider a phenomenon like the so-called Paul McCartney Death Rumor. Nearly two thousand years after Ovid composed the *Metamorphoses* (which recounts the story of the beautiful youth Hyacinth, a very literal flower-child, who was slain and subsequently resurrected in the form of the blossom which bears his name), a whole generation of flower-children—members of the counterculture and other rock music fans—were suddenly gripped by the strange conviction that one of *their* heroes, the androgynously pretty Paul McCartney, had been killed in a car accident and then miraculously reborn (in the form of an exact duplicate who looked and sang exactly like, or even better than, the original). This rumor is clearly incredible, and the fact that it was believed by so many people cannot be understood in logical terms, though it can be understood in mythological ones, as the recurrence of an archetypal idea.

The popularity of the Beatles is in itself a striking sign of the emergence of the myth of the child, because the Beatles were the supreme embodiments of the archetype, and their phenomenal popularity demonstrates the dominance of that symbol during most of the sixties. John, Paul, George and Ringo, the four mop-tops, were eternal children turned into flesh and art. They were the minstrels of the *puer* state of mind. In his book *Gates of Eden,* Morris Dickstein discusses the "irrepressibly childlike qualities of the Beatles." He describes their "exuberance and effervescence," their "incurable addiction to the pleasure principle," and the "childlike magic" which was so "central to their appeal."[12] The very titles of their songs reveal the group's childlike sensibility: "Yellow Submarine," "Octopus's Garden," "Mother Nature's Son" (which might have been the theme song of Attis or Tammuz), etc. As Dickstein notes, "Lennon's lyrics are sometimes so simple they look like the children's nonsense verse, which he also writes very well."[13] And Paul McCartney, after leaving the group and forming Wings, even recorded a version of "Mary Had a Little Lamb."

The retreat into the world of the child is evident everywhere in the counterculture. There are, for example, the costumes adopted by the "love children." In *Loose Change,* her vivid evocation of the sixties, Sara Davidson describes the guests at a party she attended in Berkeley in 1967: "They were wearing Edwardian velvet gowns, spaceman suits, African robes, cowboy regalia, Donald Duck hats and Indian war paint."[14] Like kids preparing for Halloween or playing with a trunkful of outlandish clothes they have discovered in their grandparents's attic, the hippies loved to dress up.

They also loved bright colors. To recall the sixties is to conjure up a world of posters, light shows, psychedelic art, and supergraphics—an explosion of radiant primary colors.

Toys were another standard feature of the sixties counterculture. The frisbee fad started back in the sixties. "Head shops" did a big business in kaleidoscopes, prisms, reflecting disks of various sorts, and something which has since disappeared from the market but which enjoyed a good deal of popularity during those psychedelic days—an item called "Ocean in a Bottle," which consisted of a clear plastic cylinder filled with a viscous blue fluid. When the cylinder was tilted back and forth, the fluid recreated the motion of ocean waves.

Like most of the optical toys popular during the sixties, "Ocean in a Bottle" was intended primarily for the enjoyment of people who were stoned (since there is a limited amount of pleasure a sober person can derive from watching some blue liquid slosh back and forth in a container). Drugs—obviously a central feature of the sixties counterculture—were another manifestation of the myth which that generation was caught up in, an expression of what Hillman and von Franz describe as ascensionism: the desire "to get as high as possible." According to von Franz, people characterized by the *puer* psychology are very attracted to such activities as mountaineering and aviation. But, as Harry Chapin points out in his popular song "Taxi" (in which a young man, who had dreamt of becoming a pilot but ended up driving a cab, "flies" instead by getting stoned), there is more than one way to get high.

The desire to drop out—the refusal to enter time, history or society—is very evident in the sixties, an era in which people were urged to "Turn on, tune in, drop out." Another popular slogan of the time, "Never trust anyone over thirty," captures the corollary of the desire to remain a child: namely, the fear of aging and distrust of adults. The same sentiment is powerfully expressed in The Who's anthem, "My Generation," containing the lyric, "Hope I die before I get old"—which is of course simply another way of saying, "I'll Never Grow Up."

The latter song, "I'll Never Grow Up," comes from the 1950s television production of *Peter Pan*, whose title character is a perfect popular representation of the *puer aeternus* archetype. He refuses to grow up, lives with his tribe of lost boys in Never Never Land (an earlier version of Strawberry Fields), has the ability to fly, and so on. Also, interestingly, in both TV versions of *Peter Pan*, the title role is played by women—Mary Martin in the 1950s and Mia Farrow in the more recent production. There is something distinctly androgynous about Peter Pan. Androgyny is a trait of the *puer aeternus*—and again, we see this in the sixties in the move toward what used to be called "unisex."[15]

A related phenomenon is the change in sexual behavior which took place in the sixties, specifically a shift to the kind of infantile or "polymorphous perverse" sexuality, which Norman O. Brown defines as "the pursuit of pleasure obtained through the activity of any and all organs of the human body."[16] We find, for example, a marked fascination with—even fixation on—oral lovemaking; an emphasis on "getting in touch with your body," which produces phenomena like the Esalen Institute in California and various "see me, feel me, touch me, hear me" therapies, the "group grope" (as the rock group The Fugs used to say), and so on.

The fear of being pinned down which von Franz describes—and the wanderlust and restlessness which go along with it—can be seen clearly in the prevalence of what might be called "the highway fantasy": dozens of films and songs about "movin' along the highway" (in the words of Carole King). It is a fantasy perhaps best exemplified by the movie *Easy Rider* and some of the early lyrics of Bob Dylan, whose second album is called *The Freewheelin' Bob Dylan* (a later release is titled *Highway 61 Revisited*). This fantasy (which the comedian Steve Martin parodies with his "I'm a ramblin' guy" pose) is closely related to another *puer* trait—the fear of being trapped in a relationship. Once again, Bob Dylan's music provides the prime expression of this feeling, particularly the song "Don't Think Twice It's All Right," in which the singer tells his lover, "When the rooster crows at the break of dawn / Look out your window and I'll be gone."

As for the holy innocent (or holy fool): this part of the *puer* sensibility is also prevalent in the sixties. The Beatles' "Fool on the Hill" is probably the purest expression of it in rock, though it is also strikingly present in the lyrics of Paul Simon (see, for example, "Save the Life of My Child," "Punky's Dilemma," "Papa Hobo," "Duncan," and "Loves Me Like a Rock") and in the persona of Arlo Guthrie in "Alice's Restaurant." In literature, it informs the fiction of Kurt Vonnegut (particularly *Slaughterhouse-Five, or, The Children's Crusade)*, Richard Brautigan and Joseph Heller. Benjamin Braddock, the hero of the movie *The Graduate* (an important film of the period) is a perfect example of the holy innocent who is regarded as a fool because he doesn't share the materialistic values of his elders: he isn't interested in spending his life in plastics.[17]

The trickster element of the counterculture has been discussed in a provocative article by E. Allen Tilley, who sees the trickster as the dominant myth of the sixties.[18] While Tilley puts too much emphasis on the trickster—which is just one aspect of the larger myth of the time—he does an excellent job of describing its appearance in such phenomena as the Yippies and Ken Kesey's Merry Pranksters. In the popular arts, the prime embodiments of this aspect of the *puer aeternus* archetype are undoubtedly the Rolling Stones, the Peck's Bad Boys of rock. The hit movie *Animal House*, as I suggested earlier, is faithful to the trickster spirit of the sixties (though the film is set rather anachronistically in the early years of the decade).

The feeling for or closeness to nature that is part of the *puer* myth is obvious in the sixties counterculture. The sixties are the time when the back-to-nature movement begins to blossom in this country; when the nation's ecology-consciousness begins to be raised; when masses of Americans start dreaming about returning to the land—and many make the attempt; when plant stores and health food stores start popping up in every neighborhood and "all natural" products suddenly fill the supermarket shelves.

Related to this new prominence of Mother Nature is the phenomenon Hillman describes: the tendency to divinize or demonize the parents. If one examines fairy tales or children's literature in general, one sees very clearly the child's habit of mythologizing adults, of perceiving them as monumental beings. Mothers may be wicked witches or helpful fairy godmothers; fathers may be cannibalistic ogres or giants (as in "Jack and the Beanstalk") or beneficent Wise Old Men. Once again, when we look at the sixties we find the same fantasy figures dominating the imagination of the counterculture. We find Mother Nature making a comeback, reverenced in various forms of behavior, from vegetarianism to the ecology movement, and celebrated in poetry, music and elsewhere. A perfect statement of this feeling for nature is the song "Mother Earth," written by Eric Kaz and recorded by Tom Rush in his album *Merrimack County:*

While Mother Earth looks after me

I will follow faithfully

*   *   *

I am blessed with her devotion
Mother Earth provides for me.

(These lyrics also express a theme which Jungians call "the provisional life"—the childlike fantasy that all our needs will be provided for us by a great, benevolent power, so that we need not worry about working to support ourselves.) The Beatles are also, predictably, celebrants of the Good Mother, in songs like "Lucy in the Sky with Diamonds," "Mother Nature's Son," and especially "Let It Be": "When I find myself in times of trouble / Mother Mary comes to me...."

As for the Terrible Mother, her image appears everywhere in the sixties. Ken Kesey, an important figure during this decade, portrays a very powerful Terrible Mother figure in his novel *One Flew Over the Cuckoo's Nest:* the monstrous "Big Nurse" Ratched. She also appears in *The Graduate,* in the character Mrs. Robinson. Comic books, song lyrics, T-shirts and posters all proclaimed the ascendance of Kali, whose symbol—the ravening mouth with its obscenely jutting tongue—became even more pervasive after its adoption by the Rolling Stones. This move by the Stones was not very surprising. If the Beatles celebrated the Good Mother and sang "Let it Be," the Stones could be counted on to celebrate the Terrible Mother and sing "Let it Bleed."

Similarly, as soon as the Beatles released an album (*Sgt. Pepper's Lonely Hearts Club Band*) dedicated in spirit to their Good Father figure, the Maharishi, the Stones rushed out an album dedicated to the Terrible Father: to "His Satanic Majesty." The tendency of the counterculture to create Good Father figures, Wise Old Men, can be seen not only in the sudden celebrity of the Maharishi but also in the prominence of all the gurus of the day— Timothy Leary, Baba Ram Dass and so on (indeed, it is in the sixties that the word "guru" becomes a part of our everyday speech). As for the flip side of the myth, the Negative Father who destroys his children: he too appears repeatedly in the sixties, in the fantasy of the hard-hat killer (the best example of which is probably the popular movie *Joe*, in which the title character ends up shooting his own hippie daughter) and in the fantasy/reality of LBJ and Nixon, who, in this mythic age, play out the mythic role of the Terrible Father-Destroyer of children.

Destroying children, in fact, has a great deal to do with why the *puer aeternus* myth arose in the first place, as I will explain in a moment.

3

But first, let me summarize: I have tried to show that the dominant myth of the sixties was that of the eternal child—that the pyschological traits associated with this myth were precisely the ones lived out by the counterculture. The question then becomes: what caused this particular myth to emerge when it did?

It seems to me that if we look at American society between World War II and the Vietnam War, when the flower-child generation was being born, growing up and coming of age, we see a society which is militaristic, increasingly mechanized and technologized, which prizes competitiveness and masculine aggression, defines sex roles very rigidly and so forth. Following Jung's theory of archetypal compensation, we can say, I believe, that the counterculture was given shape and direction by unconscious forces operating on a collective scale and with a particular purpose (because, as I have explained, the unconscious, according to Jung, *is* purposive; it does have a definite aim, which is self-regulation, the maintenance of psychic health and balance). During the sixties, as in other eras, the unconscious strove to achieve this purpose by raising the symbol of the neglected values into the cultural consciousness of mainstream American society, by forcing the culture at large into an awareness of those values which it had been denying, to its detriment.

Symbolically speaking, the opposite of war, aggression, competition, death-machinery, is the eternal child. (Hence, many anti-war posters used the baby or child as an image of peace during the sixties, and a popular slogan of the time went "War isn't healthy for children and other living things." The same antithesis of childhood and war can be seen clearly in the hit movie *M*A*S*H,* in which the reaction to war is a retreat into the child/trickster behavior of its heroes, Hawkeye and Trapper John, and in which the best people are holy innocents like Radar O'Reilly.) The denial of child-values by American society—and the actual destruction of children (an image bombarding us daily through the mass media)—led to a compensatory reaction among the young, an exaltation of those values which American society seemed intent on destroying.

To be sure, it's clear—in fact, glaringly obvious—that the values and behavior of the counterculture were counter to those of the mainstream culture. But it is my contention that the shape and destiny of the counterculture were determined by deeply unconscious forces; that it was a mass movement created and motivated first and foremost by unconscious compulsions (only later was the role of the child adopted as a conscious stance and strategy). It is possible, of course, to look at the sixties counterculture and see its retreat into childhood as merely regressive and infantile behavior: a large-scale neurosis. But, while there is an element of truth to this, it's a mistake to see the counterculture as nothing more than a symptom.

Jung teaches us to look at neuroses, not symptomatically, but symbolically. The counterculture *was* a symptom of a cultural sickness; but it was also the living symbol of the cure, a push toward a new synthesis—an attempt (ironically) to set American society straight.

Notes

Introduction

[1]Joseph Campbell, *Myths to Live By* (New York: Bantam Books, 1973), p. 24.

[2]Stan Lee, *Origins of Marvel Comics* (New York: Simon and Schuster, 1974), p. 18.

[3]Quoted by Robert Jewett and John Shelton Lawrence in *The American Monomyth* (Garden City, New York: Anchor Press/Doubleday, 1977), p. 2.

[4]*The American Monomyth*, p. 226.

[5]Ibid., pp. 23 ff. Two other critics have commented on the religious quality of *Star Trek*. In an article in the *Journal of Popular Culture*, Wm. Blake Tyrell discusses the mythic significance of the series and concludes that "*Star Trek* offers the comfort of religion." ("*Star Trek* as Myth and Television as Mythmaker," *Journal of Popular Culture*, 10, 1977, pp. 711-719.) And Andrew Greeley, writing in the "Arts and Leisure" section of the Sunday *New York Times*, compares *Star Trek* "to the Medieval morality plays (Captain Kirk as Everyman)." Greeley's thesis in this article is similar to my own—that popular culture has assumed one of the roles played in the past by organized religion—though Greeley draws his evidence entirely from the current craze for science fiction films: "The churches have given up Wonder for such things as instant political relevance and bargain-basement psychology, so science fiction moves into the vacuum with a dazzling array of marvelous events and an army of Wonder Creatures.... With the coming of science as a secular religion it was bequeathed that there was no more room in the cosmos for the miraculous.... But you can't demythologize the hunger for the wonderful out of the human personality...." ("When Religion Cast Off Wonder, Hollywood Seized It," *New York Times*, 27 November 1977, Sec. 2, pp. 1 and 11.)

[6]*The American Monomyth*, p. 23. A bit later on in their book, Jewett and Lawrence make note of "the crazy antics of movie star fans and rock fans" and observe that "the religious quality of such behavior has not been taken seriously, in part because of the artifacts of popular culture that inspire such behavior are not explicitly religious" (34). This is an important insight and one which was verified in an interesting way when, shortly after his death, CBS television broadcast a taping of Elvis Presley's last concert. Periodically during his performance, Elvis would stroll back and forth across the stage and pass white silk scarves down to the delirious audience. As soon as he had disposed of one scarf, a retainer carrying an armful of them would drape another across his neck, where the "king" would let it hang for a moment before bestowing it on some hysterical fan. Several nights later, on a different network, a nearly identical scene was televised—only this time, the program was a documentary on revivalist preaching, and the protagonist was not a rock star but a camp-meeting evangelist, pressing "prayer-cloths" into the hands of his frenzied followers. The two scenes

paralleled each other in a truly striking—and instructive—way. (The close connection between religion and rock is embodied in the person of Marjoe Gortner, a young evangelist who, by his own admission, brought the gestures of Mick Jagger to his preaching style, and who has, during the past few years, abandoned his ministry for a career as a popular entertainer.)

[7]Mircea Eliade, *Myths, Dreams, and Mysteries,* trans. Philip Mairet (New York: Harper & Row/Harper Colophon Books, 1975), p. 27.

[8]Alan McGlashan, "Daily Paper Pantheon: A New Fantasia of the Unconscious," *The Lancet,* 31 Jan. 1953, pp. 238-239.

[9]*Myths to Live By,* p. 24.

[10]Edward G. Cohen, *C.G. Jung and the Scientific Attitude* (New York: Philosophical Library, 1975), p. 33.

[11]C.G. Jung, "The Concept of the Collective Unconscious," in *The Archetypes and the Collective Unconscious, Collected Works,* IX, part 1, trans. R.F.C. Hull (Princeton: Princeton University Press/Bollingen Series XX, 1959), pp. 51-52.

[12]Jung, "Commentary on *The Secret of the Golden Flower,*" in *Alchemical Studies, C.W.* XII, p. 11.

[13]Jung, "The Structure of the Psyche," in *The Structure and Dynamics of the Psyche, C.W.* VIII, pp. 152 and 158.

[14]Joseph Campbell, *The Masks of God: Primitive Mythology* (New York: The Viking Press, 1970), p. 31.

[15]*The Masks of God,* p. 35.

[16]Jung, "On the Nature of the Psyche," *C.W.* VIII, p. 201.

[17]*C.W.* VIII, p. 201.

[18]*Two Essays on Analytical Psychology, C.W.* p.190.

[19]Campbell, *The Masks of God,* p. 37.

[20]Jung, "Instinct and the Unconscious," *C.W.* VIII, p. 136.

[21]"On the Nature of the Psyche," *C.W.* VIII, p. 201.

[22]*C.W.*VII, pp. 178 and 149.

[23]Jung, *Contributions to Analytical Psychology,* trans. H.G. and Cary Baynes (London: Kegan Paul Trench and Trubner & Co., 1928), p. 246.

[24]Erich Neumann, *The Great Mother: An Analysis of the Archetype,* trans. Ralph Manheim (Princeton: Princeton University Press/Bollingen Series XLVII, 1972), p. 15.

[25]"On the Psychology of the Trickster-Figure," *C.W.* IX, part 1, p. 260.

[26]*Anatomy of Criticism* (Princeton: Princeton University Press, 1957), p. 116.

[27]From the text of an address delivered at the third national meeting of the Popular Culture Association and subsequently published in *The Spectrum,* the student newspaper of the State University of New York at Buffalo, 18 April 1975, 5-6.

[28]"Myth and Archetype in Science Fiction," *Parabola,* I, no. 4 (Fall 1976), p. 45.

[29]Jung himself compares *She* to *Moby-Dick* but in doing so avoids all aesthetic judgments: "There is a fundamental difference of attitude between the psychologist's approach to a literary work and that of a literary critic," he maintains. "What is of decisive importance for the latter might be quite irrelevant for the former" ("Psychology and Literature," in *The Spirit in Man, Art, and*

Literature, C.W. XV, p. 87.)

Chapter One

¹Erich Neumann, *The Great Mother: An Analysis of the Archetype,* trans. Ralph Manheim (Princeton: Princeton University Press, 1972, Bollingen Series XLVII), p. 4.

²Ibid., pp. 8-9.

³C.G. Jung, *Symbols of Transformation, Collected Works,* V, trans.R.F.C. Hull (Princeton: Princeton University Press, 1956, Bollingen Series XX), p. 232.

⁴*Ego and Archetype: Individuation and the Religious Function of the Psyche* (Baltimore: Penguin Books, 1973), p. 130.

⁵*Hero With a Thousand Faces* (Princeton: Princeton University Press, 1972, Bollingen Series XVII), p. 30.

⁶Ibid., pp. 245-246.

⁷Jolande Jacobi, *The Psychology of C.G. Jung* (New Haven: Yale University Press, 1973), pp. 108-109.

⁸John Halverson, "The Shadow in *Moby-Dick,*" *American Quarterly,* 15 (Fall 1963), 437.

⁹Alex Aronson, *Psyche & Symbol in Shakespeare* (Bloomington: Indiana University Press, 1972), p. 29.

¹⁰*Two Essays on Analytical Psychology, C.W.* VII, p. 178.

¹¹Gerhard Adler, *The Living Symbol: A Case Study in the Process of Individuation* (Princeton: Princeton University Press/Pantheon Books, 1961, Bollingen Series LXII), p.60.

¹²M. Esther Harding, "What makes the symbol effective as a healing agent?" in *Current Trends in Analytical Psychology: Proceedings of the First International Congress for Analytical Psychology,* ed. Gerhard Adler (London: Tavistock Publications, 1961), p. 14.

¹³*Hero With a Thousand Faces,* p. 9.

¹⁴Jolande Jacobi, *The Way of Individuation,* trans. R.F.C. Hull (New York: Harcourt, Brace & World, 1967), p. 17.

¹⁵Ibid., p. 28.

¹⁶Jung, "On the Nature of Dreams," *C.W.* VIII, pp. 290-291.

¹⁷Jung, "Psychology and Literature," in *Modern Man in Search of a Soul,* trans. W.S. Dell and Cary F. Baynes (New York: Harcourt, Brace & World/Harvest Books, 1933), pp. 152-172.

¹⁸*Hero With a Thousand Faces,* pp. 17-18.

¹⁹*Ego and Archetype,* p. 131.

²⁰New York: Spring Publications, 1970, section I, pp. 1-2.

²¹Kirsch,"The Enigma of Moby Dick," *Journal of Analytical Psychology,* 3, (1958),131-147; Halverson, "The Shadow in *Moby-Dick,*" *American Quarterly,* 15 (Fall 1963), 436-446; Pops, *The Melville Archetype* (Kent, Ohio: Kent State University Press, 1970); Edinger, *Melville's* Moby Dick: *A Jungian Commentary/An American Nekyia* (New York: New Directions, 1978).

²²See Pops, *The Melville Archetype,* p. 4.

²³"Psychology and Literature," in *The Spirit in Man, Art and Literature, C.W.*

XV, p. 88.

[24]New York: Hillstone-Stonehill, 1967, pp. 18-19.

[25]Ibid., p. 23.

[26]February, 1973. One problem in talking about comic books in a critical study is that many readers will inevitably be unfamiliar with the particular stories under discussion and won't be able to look them up in a library. The only solution is for the author to describe the work as fully as he can and, possibly, to reproduce a few panels. The case of "In the Beginning" is somewhat different, however, since Jonna Gormely Semeiks and I have reprinted the story in its entirety in our textbook, *Patterns in Popular Culture* (New York: Harper & Row, 1980), to which interested readers are referred.

[27] See Bruno Bettelheim, *The Uses of Enchantment* (New York: Knopf, 1976), p. 5.

[28]E. Nelson Bridwell, author, editor, and comic book scholar, has informed me that the lawsuit originally instituted by National was actually won by Fawcett. National then reopened the case, but it never came to trial because Fawcett, which by that time was losing money on the Captain Marvel line, decided not to spend more on another lengthy court battle and offered National an out-of-court cash settlement instead.

[29]Bettelheim, p. 217.

[30]From an unpublished essay, "The Water of Life: Fairy Tale and the Ritual of Self-Discovery."

[31]*Love and Death in the American Novel* (New York: Dell Publishing Company/Delta Books, 1966), p. 160.

[32]*The Masks of God: Primitive Mythology* (New York: The Viking Press, 1970), pp. 68-69.

[33]Jung, *Psychology and Alchemy, C.W.* XII, p. 58.

[34]Northrop Frye, "New Directions from Old," in *Myth and Mythmaking*, ed. Henry A. Murray (Boston: Beacon Press, 1968), pp. 127-128.

[35]E. Nelson Bridwell has pointed out to me that in the story "King Kull and the Seven Sins" (*Captain Marvel Adventures*, no. 137, Oct. 1952), these statues are brought to life by black magic and are actually referred to as "The Seven Deadly Sins."

[36]Lupoff's remark, which stands as the epigraph to section two, comes from his essay "The Big Red Cheese," in *All in Color for a Dime*, ed. Dick Lupoff and Don Thompson (New York: Ace Books, 1970), p. 64. Ten years ago or so, I attended a concert by the rock group The Fugs, in the course of which singer Ken Weaver described God as an "old guy in a long white robe who looks like Shazam."

[37]A story entitled "The Marvel Family Reaches Eternity" (from *Marvel Family*, no. 7, Dec. 1946)—which E. Nelson Bridwell has kindly called to my attention—confirms my interpretation of the contents of "The Ancient Book of Shazam." Inscribed in the volume is a message about "The Book of Eternity," which reveals that in his immaterial state, Shazam sits on "the rock of eternity," "recording the history of the Marvel family"—whom, I believe, we are meant to take as Everyman figures. In effect, then, Shazam, like God, inhabits an eternal realm, from the vantage point of which he keeps a record of the history of the family of man.

³⁸See Murray, pp. 128-130.

³⁹*The Masks of God: Primitive Mythology*, p. 185.

⁴⁰*Hero With a Thousand Faces*, p. 246.

⁴¹*The Great Comic Book Heroes* (New York: The Dial Press, 1965), p. 25.

⁴²*Hero With a Thousand Faces*, pp. 136-137. In the story "The Son of Shazam" (*Whiz Comics*, no. 105, Jan. 1949), the ancient wizard reveals that Captain Marvel is in fact his son. My thanks, once again, to E. Nelson Bridwell for pointing this out to me.

⁴³Campbell, *The Masks of God: Primitive Mythology*, pp. 88-131; Howitt, *The Native Tribes of South-East Australia* (London: Macmillan, 1909); Van Gennep, *The Rites of Passage*, trans. Monika B. Vizedom and Gabrielle L. Caffee (Chicago: University of Chicago Press, 1960); Eliade, *Rites and Symbols of Initiation*, trans. William R. Trask (New York: Harper & Row/Harper Torchbooks, 1965); Bettelheim, *Symbolic Wounds* (New York: Collier Books, 1962). See also Edward Clodd, *Magic in Names and Other Things* (New York: Dutton, 1921), pp. 83-88.

⁴⁴"Superman to the Rescue!" *Newsweek*, 1 Jan. 1979, pp. 46-51.

⁴⁵*Love and Death in the American Novel*, p. 24.

⁴⁶"Come Back to the Raft Ag'in, Huck Honey," in *An End to Innocence* (Boston: Beacon Press, 1955), p. 144.

⁴⁷See *Psychology and Alchemy, C.W. XII*, pp.108n, 131, 428.

⁴⁸*Aion, C.W. IX*, part II, p. 40.

⁴⁹See Frederic Wertham, *Seduction of the Innocent* (New York: Rinehart, 1954), pp. 188-193.

⁵⁰"Ritual transformation into a woman" is discussed by Eliade, *Rites and Symbols of Initiation*, p. 26; Bettelheim, *Symbolic Wounds*, p. 54; and Robert H. Lowie, *Primitive Society* (New York: Horace Liveright, 1920), p. 272.

⁵¹*The Archetypes and The Collective Unconscious, C.W. IX*, part I, p. 21.

Chapter Two

¹*An Introduction to Jung's Psychology* (Baltimore: Penguin Books, 1970), pp. 49-50.

²"The Archetypes of the Collective Unconscious," *C.W. IX*, part I, p. 20.

³Halverson, 437.

⁴Ibid., 436.

⁵Jung,"Concerning Rebirth," *C.W. IX*, part I, p. 138.

⁶Jung, *Symbols of Transformation, C.W.V*, p. 183.

⁷Herman Melville, *Moby-Dick*, ed. Harrison Hayford and Hershel Parker (New York: Norton Critical Editions, 1967), p. 16.

⁸Ibid., pp. 12 and 53.

⁹*A Primer of Jungian Psychology* (New York: New American Library/A Mentor Book, 1973), p. 49.

¹⁰V, i, 275-276.

¹¹*Virgin Land* (New York: Random House/Vintage Books, 1950), pp. 100-101.

¹²Cf. the climax of Conrad's "The Secret Sharer," where the young narrator, having confronted and befriended his shadow, achieves the confidence and self-

possession he needs to take charge of his ship and steer it through danger.

[13]*A Wizard of Earthsea* (New York: Bantam Books, 1975), p. 160. Subsequent quotes in the text refer to this edition.

[14]*The Strange Case of Doctor Jekyll and Mr. Hyde, and Other Stories* (New York: Pocket Books, 1941), p. 60.

[15]*Psyche & Symbol in Shakespeare* (Bloomington, Indiana: Indiana University Press, 1972), p. 114.

[16]Goofus and Gallant conform to the popular American types Leslie Fiedler identifies as the "Good Good Boy" and the "Good Bad Boy." See *Love and Death in the American Novel*, pp. 259 ff.

[17]*Memories, Dreams, Reflections*, recorded and edited by Aniela Jaffe, trans. Richard and Clara Winston (New York: Random House/Vintage Books, 1963), p. 245.

[18]This comic book story is reprinted in its entirety in *Patterns in Popular Culture*, as is "Midnight Brings Dark Death."

[19]"Evil from the Psychological Point of View," in *Evil: Studies in Jungian Thought*, ed. the Curatorium of the C.G. Jung Institute, Zurich, trans. Ralph Manheim and Hildegaard Nagel (Evanston: Northwest University Press, 1967), p. 162.

[20]See Jolande Jacobi, *The Psychology of C.G. Jung* (New Haven: Yale University Press, 1973), p. 113.

[21]Halverson, 439.

[22]From *Zap* no. 0.

[23]*O Brave New World*, ed. Leslie Fiedler and Arthur Zeiger (New York: Dell Publishing Co., 1968), p. 26.

[24]See *Regeneration Through Violence: The Mythology of the American Frontier, 1600-1800* (Middletown, Connecticut: Wesleyan University Press, 1973).

[25]*Edgar Huntly, or, Memoirs of a Sleepwalker* (New Haven, Connecticut: College and University Press, 1973), p. 197. Subsequent references in the text are to this edition.

[26]From *The Hands of Shang-Chi, Master of Kung Fu, Special Marvel Edition*, Vol. 1, no. 16 (Feb. 1974).

[27]Paul D. Zimmerman, "Rites of Manhood," *Newsweek*, 20 Dec. 1971, p. 86.

[28]This introductory section of the novel is omitted from the film version of *Deliverance*, which opens with Ed and his companions on the way to the river. While the filmmakers' decision to limit themselves strictly to the adventure in the woods was undoubtedly a wise cinematic choice—the movie is very fast-paced and suspenseful—it also significantly altered the meaning of the original story, as did the casting of younger men in the four lead roles and the changes made in the ending (see below, n. 48).

Page references in my text are to the Dell paperback edition of *Deliverance* (New York: Dell Publishing Co., 1970).

[29]Frieda Fordham, *An Introduction to Jung's Psychology* (Baltimore: Penguin Books, 1970), p. 78.

[30]p. 31. This incident foreshadows the scene in the wilderness when Ed—confronting the unbridled terrors of the id directly—is threatened with castration by one of the mountaineers (p.98).

[31]Another possible source for Ed's surname is suggested by the poem "On the Coosawatee" (from *Helmets)*, which describes a canoe trip similar in certain respects to the one in *Deliverance* and features a character named "Lucas Gentry."

[32]C.G. Jung, *Psychology and Alchemy, Collected Works* XII, trans. R.F.C. Hull (Princeton: Princeton University Press, 1968, Bollingen Series XX), p. 137.

[33]*Thresholds of Initiation* (Middletown, Connecticut: Wesleyan University Press, 1967), p. 134.

[34]Herman Melville, *Moby-Dick,* pp. 162 and 104.

[35]Ibid., pp. 12 and 140.

[36]"Art and Immediacy: James Dickey's *Deliverance,"Southern Review,* 7, No. 3 (1971), 951.

[37]"The Harmony of Bestiality in James Dickey's *Deliverance," South Carolina Review,* 5, No. 1 (1972), 44-45.

[38]"Evil from the Psychological Point of View," p. 162.

[39]C.G. Jung, *Symbols of Transformation, C.W.* V, p. 224.

[40]Chapter VII, p. 12.

[41]"Evil from the Psychological Point of View," p. 186.

[42]Alex Aronson, *Psyche & Symbol in Shakespeare,* p. 115.

[43]"The Shadow in *Moby-Dick,"* p. 438. Cf. Leslie Fiedler's remarks about Chingachgook, Jim and Queequeg in *Love and Death in the American Novel,* esp. p. 369.

Ed's uncertainty about the slain man's identity reflects, I believe, the shadow's ambiguous nature. While the shadow figure appears totally evil before it is incorporated, it performs a positive function—and assumes a correspondingly positive image—once it is brought to consciousness. The fact that Ed cannot definitely identify the dead man does not mean that he has shot an innocent person but that his shadow, having been "realized," no longer appears as revolting as it did earlier. Peter G. Beidler points out that "the tall rapist" has "yellow-tinged eyeballs" and a totally toothless mouth, whereas the man Ed kills on the mountain has "clear blue" eyes and only a "partial upper plate." Beidler concludes that Ed "has killed the wrong man." (" 'The Pride of Thine Heart Hath Deceived Thee': Narrative Distortion in Dickey's *Deliverance," South Carolina Review,* 5, No. 1, 1973, 29-40). My contention, however, is that these physical discrepencies symbolize the shift in the shadow's nature, the "humanization of the Other."

The metamorphosis of the shadow can also be seen in Conrad's "The Secret Sharer." When Leggatt, the narrator's double, first appears, he is a terrifying apparition: "ghastly, silvery, fish-like." As the narrator becomes acquainted with him, however, Leggatt is transformed from a horror into a helpmate and friend.

[44]*Hero With a Thousand Faces,* p. 108.

[45]*Symbols of Transformation, C.W.* V, p. 218.

[46]William Shakespeare, *Hamlet,* III, iv, 20: "You go not till I set you up a glass / Where you may see the inmost part of you."

[47]C.G. Jung, *The Archetypes and the Collective Unconscious, C.W.* IX, part 1, p. 131.

[48]*Complex/Archetype/Symbol* (Princeton: Princeton University Press, 1959,

Bollingen Series LVII), p. 186.

The film version of *Deliverance* ends on a very different note: with Ed haunted by nightmares of the slain mountaineer. Unlike his counterpart in the novel, the hero of the movie is unable to accept his shadow. The film's penultimate image—of the hand of the dead man rising menacingly out of the river—suggests that Ed has only repressed his aggressive side again, and that it will reemerge from the depths of the unconscious, a continuing source of trouble and disturbance. (I should add, however, that in cinematic terms, the shot is very effective, very chilling, and that, had the ending of the movie been as serene as that of the book, it probably would have been anticlimactic. So once again—as with the omission of the prologue—the filmmakers' alteration of the original story, while drastically changing its meaning, was valid and perhaps wise, given their decision to make a simple, straightforward thriller.)

Chapter Three

[1] Jung, *The Structure and Dynamics of the Psyche, C.W.* VIII, p. 310.

[2] *The Symbolic Quest: Basic Concepts of Analytical Psychology* (New York: Harper & Row/Harper Colophon Books, 1973), pp. 161-162.

[3] Liliane Frey-Rohn, "Evil from a Psychological Point of View," in *Evil*, p. 164.

[4] *The Trickster: A Study in American Indian Mythology* (New York: Schocken Books, 1971), p. xxiii.

[5] *The Trickster*, pp. 200-207.

[6] Thomas Maremaa, "Who Is This Crumb?" *The New York Times Magazine*, 1 Oct. 1972, p. 13.

[7] Originally published in *Black and White Comics* (1973). Reprinted in *Patterns in Popular Culture*.

[8] Jung, "On the Psychology of the Trickster-Figure," in *The Trickster*, pp. 206 and 196.

[9] See Paul Buhle, "The New Comics and American Culture," *TriQuarterly*, 23/24 (Winter/Spring 1972), 380.

[10] Ibid.

[11] *The Trickster*, p. 200.

[12] Ibid., p. 201.

[13] Ibid., p. 203.

[14] *Hero With a Thousand Faces*, p. 45.

[15] *The Trickster*, pp. 29-30.

[16] Ibid., p. 195.

[17] Nicholas Udall, *Ralph Roister Doister*, in *Minor Elizabethan Drama*, Volume Two (London: Everyman's Library, 1964), p. 5.

[18] In *A Treasury of American Folklore*, ed. B.A. Botkin (Garden City, N.Y.: Garden City Books, 1951), pp. 667-668.

[19] Set in 1962, *Animal House* is somewhat anachronistic, portraying as it does anti-establishment attitudes and behavior (smoking pot at a "hip" professor's home, for example) more characteristic of the late sixties college generation. In

depicting its heroes as archetypal tricksters, however, the filmmakers have captured an essential element of the countercultural sensibility. For more on the connection between the counterculture and the trickster, see the Appendix.

[20]*The Trickster,* p. 202.

[21]Peter Mayle, *Baby Taming* (New York: Crown Publishers, 1979).

[22]*Love and Death in the American Novel,* p. 207.

[23]George W. Peck, *Peck's Bad Boy and His Pa* (Chicago: John R. Stanton Co, 1883), pp. 42-44.

[24]For a complete and characteristically provocative discussion of this myth, see Leslie Fiedler, *The Return of the Vanishing American* (New York: Stein and Day, 1969), pp. 97-108.

[25]*Peck's Bad Boy and His Pa,* p. 28.

[26]Edgar Allan Poe, "The Imp of the Perverse," in *Complete Stories and Poems of Edgar Allan Poe* (Garden City, New York: Doubleday & Co., 1968), p. 274.

[27]Joseph Campbell, *The Masks of God: Primitive Mythology,* p. 273.

[28]Ibid., p. 274.

[29]Frederic Wertham, *Seduction of the Innocent* (New York: Rinehart & Co., 1954), p. 239.

[30]Ibid., pp. 240, 241.

[31]Bruno Bettelheim, *The Uses of Enchantment,* pp. 76, 78.

[32]Heinrich Zimmer, *The King and the Corpse: Tales of the Soul's Conquest of Evil,* ed. Joseph Campbell (Princeton: Princeton University Press/Bollingen Series XI, 1971), pp. 38-39.

[33]Ibid., p. 38.

[34]Stith Thompson, *The Folktale* (New York: Holt, Rinehart & Winston, 1946), p. 59.

[35]Donald McQuade and Robert Atwan, *Popular Writing in America* (New York: Oxford University Press, 1974), p. 219.

[36]See, for example, the story of Prince which figures importantly in Peter Shaffer's play *Equus* (New York: Avon/Bard Books, 1974), pp. 35-36.

Chapter Four

[1]*Two Essays on Analytical Psychology, C.W.* VII, p. 211.

[2]"The Vision of the Fountain," in *The Complete Short Stories of Nathaniel Hawthorne* (New York: Hanover House, 1959), p. 106.

[3]*C.W.* IX, part 1, pp. 24-25.

[4]*The Symbolic Quest,* p. 192.

[5]*C.W.* VII, p. 189.

[6]Jolande Jacobi, *The Psychology of C.G. Jung* (New Haven: Yale Univeristy Press, 1973), p. 119.

[7]"The Process of Individuation," in *Man and His Symbols,* ed. C.G. Jung (New York: Dell Publishing Co., 1971), p. 119.

[8]Emma Jung, *Anima and Animus* (Zurich: Spring Publications, 1972), p. 53.

[9]*Deliverance,* pp. 21-22.

[10]Joseph L. Henderson, *Thresholds of Initiation* (Middletown, Connecticut:

Wesleyan University Press, 1967), p. 61, and June Singer, *Boundaries of the Soul* (Garden City, N.Y.: Anchor Press/Doubleday, 1973), p. 239.

[11]*The Great Mother,* p. 33.

[12]*The Living Symbol,* p. 166.

[13]Introduction to *Conan* by Robert E. Howard (London: Sphere Books, Ltd., 1974), p. 10.

[14]Roy Thomas and Barry Smith, *The Complete Marvel Conan the Barbarian,* Vol. II (New York: Grossett & Dunlap/A Tempo Star Book, 1978).

[15]*Conan the Barbarian,* Vol. 1, no. 32 (Nov. 1973).

[16]See "Archetypes of the Collective Unconscious," *C.W.* IX, part 1, p. 25.

[17]See *Man, Myth & Magic: An Illustrated Encyclopedia of the Supernatural,* Vol. 12, ed. Richard Cavendish (New York: Marshall Cavendish Corporation, 1970), p. 1631. Also, see Wolfgang Lederer, *The Fear of Women* (New York: Harcourt Brace Jovanovich/A Harvest Book, 1968), p. 61; and Merlin Stone, *When God Was a Woman* (New York: Harcourt Brace Jovanovich/A Harvest Book, 1978), pp. 158-159.

[18]Bram Stoker, *Dracula* (New York: New American Library/Signet, 1965), pp. 46-47.

[19]Sanger D. Shafer and Lefty Frizzell, "Bandy the Rodeo Clown," copyright 1975 by Acuff-Rose Publications, Inc.

[20]*C.W.* IX, part 1, p. 30.

[21]C.G. Jung, *Analytical Psychology: Its Theory & Practice* (New York: Random House/A Pantheon Book, 1968), p. 20.

[22]See Jung's remarks on H. Rider Haggard's *She, C.W.* IX, part 1, p. 30.

[23]"Rappaccini's Daughter," in *The Complete Short Stories of Nathaniel Hawthorne,* p. 261.

[24]*An Introduction to Jung's Psychology.,* p. 54.

[25]Ibid., p. 88.

[26]*The Symbolic Quest,* pp. 20-23.

[27]*The Psychology of C.G. Jung,* p. 102.

[28]*The Great Mother,* p. xlii.

[29]*Journal of American Culture,* II (Summer 1979), p. 245.

[30]"Hollywood's New Ideal of Masculinity," *New York Times,* 16 July 1978, Sec. 2, pp. 1 and 26.

[31]Robert Bly, *Sleepers Joining Hands* (New York: Harper & Row, 1973), pp. 32-33.

[32]*The Great Mother,* p. xlii.

[33]C.G. Jung, "Psychology and Literature," in *Modern Man in Search of a Soul,* p. 166.

[34]*Screw,* no. 200, 15 Jan. 1973, pp. 6-7.

[35]*Screw,* no. 174, 3 July 1972, p. 21.

[36]In an interview in *Rolling Stone,* no. 89 (19 August 1971), Keith Richard points out that the Rolling Stones' mouth trademark is also the symbol of Kali: "All those people are as important as we are. Especially now that we've got Rolling Stones records, with the Kali tongue....nobody's gotten into that yet, but that's Kali, the Hindu female goddess" (p. 28).

[37]*The Great Mother,* p. 170.

[38]"Bang a Gong (Get It On)" by Marc Bolan. From *Electric Warrior.*

[39]In an article called "Sharks: The Making of a Bestseller," originally published in *The New York Times Magazine,* Ted Morgan reports that the original cover idea for the novel *Jaws*—a set of colossal, bleached shark's jaws framing "a peaceful unsuspecting town"—had to be abandoned because salesmen who previewed the jacket were made uneasy by it. "It made them think of Freud's classic dream of the *vagina dentata,*" writes Morgan. (*New York Times Magazine,* April 21, 1974. Reprinted in Robert Atwan et al., *American Mass Media* [New York: Random House, 1978], pp. 140-150).

[40]The first of these views—that disaster movies pander to a bloodthirsty public—is the most common and can be found in many reviews of these films. The latter interpretation is put forth by Robert Jewett and John Shelton Lawrence in *The American Monomyth.*

[41]*Heresies,* Spring 1978.

[42]From an unpublished essay, "The Birth Dance: An Ancient Matriarchal Fertility Ritual."

[43]Portions of Daniela Gioseffi's poems are used by permission of the author and are taken from her book *Eggs in the Lake* (Brockport, New York: BOA Editions, 1979).

[44]See Jung, "Concerning the Archetypes and the Anima Concept," *C.W.* IX, part 1, p. 64.

Chapter Five

[1]From *Your Hytone Comix,* 1971.

[2]C.G. Jung, "The Structure of the Psyche," *C.W.* VIII, p. 152.

[3]Alan McGlashan, "Daily Paper Pantheon."

[4]*Hero With a Thousand Faces,* p. 21. All page numbers in my text refer to this edition.

[5]Cf. Campbell. "The agony of breaking through personal limitations is the agony of spiritual growth. Art, literature, myth and cult, philosophy, and ascetic disciplines are instruments to help the individual past his limiting horizons into spheres of ever-expanding realization. As he crosses threshold after threshold, conquering dragon after dragon, the stature of the divinity he summons to his highest wish increases, until it subsumes the cosmos. Finally, the mind breaks the bounding sphere of the cosmos to a realization transcending all experiences of form—all symbolizations, all divinities: a realization of the ineluctable void" (*Hero,* p. 190).

[6]Heinrich Zimmer, *The King and the Corpse,* p. 41.

[7]Liliane Frey-Rohn, "Evil from the Psychological Point of View," in *Evil,* pp. 185, 187-188.

[8]Henry David Thoreau, *Walden* (New York: New American Library/Signet, 1960), p. 214.

[9]Joseph Campbell, *The Masks of God: Primitive Mythology,* p. 333.

[10]J.R.R. Tolkien, *The Fellowship of the Ring* (New York: Ballantine Books, 1965), p. 488.

[11]C.G. Jung, "Approaching the Unconscious," in *Man and His Symbols* (New

York: Dell Publishing Co./Laurel, 1971), p. 49.

[12]Joseph Campbell, Introduction to *The Portable Jung* (New York: The Viking Press, 1971), p. xxvi.

[13]Ibid., p. xxvii.

[14]Nathaniel Hawthorne, "The Birthmark," in *The Celestial Railroad and Other Stories* (New York: The New American Library/Signet, 1963), p. 209. Like Scotty, Aminadab is distinguished by his mechanical aptitude: "Forthwith there issued from an inner apartment a man of low stature, but bulky frame, with shaggy hair hanging about his visage, which was grimed with the vapors of the furnace. This personage had been Aylmer's underworker during his whole scientific career, and was admirably fitted for that office by his great mechanical readiness, and the skill with which... he executed all the details of his masters' experiments."

[15]The ability of archetypal patterns to take possession of a person's life is discussed in greater detail in the appendix.

[16]My thanks to Nathalie Schulyer Hayes, whose provocative, unpublished essay on sixties rock music helped start me thinking about the archetypal significance of the Beatles.

[17]Bruno Bettelheim, *The Uses of Enchantment,* p. 78.

Appendix

[1]Joseph Campbell, *Hero With a Thousand Faces*, p. 19.

[2]Joseph Campbell, *Introduction to The Portable Jung*, p. xxii.

[3]Ibid.

[4]C.G. Jung, "The Psychology of the Child Archetype," in *The Archetypes and the Collective Unconscious, C.W.* IX, part 1, p. 156.

[5]This is made explicit in *The Front*, the 1977 movie about the McCarthy era, which ends with Frank Sinatra's voice singing over the closing credits, "Fairy tales can come true / It can happen to you...." ("Young at Heart").

[6]Morris Dickstein, *Gates of Eden: American Culture in the Sixties* (New York: Basic Books, 1977), p. ix.

[7]Marie-Louise von Franz, *The Problem of the Puer Aeternus* (Zurich: Spring Publications, 1970), Section I, p. 1.

[8]James Hillman also points out that "students of literature would find the *puer* perhaps in St. Exupery, in Shelley, Rimbaud, in Rousseau; Shakespeare's Hotspur is an example; Herman Melville has at least five such beautiful sailor-wanderers." See "Pothos: The Nostalgia of the *Puer Aeternus*," in *Loose Ends: Primary Papers in Archetypal Psychology* (Zurich: Spring Publications, 1975), 49-62.

[9]Ibid., p. 50.

[10]Norman O. Brown, *Life Against Death* (Middletown, Connecticut: Wesleyan University Press, 1959), p. 24.

[11]*The Problem of the Puer Aeternus*, Section I, p. 2.

[12]*Gates of Eden*, pp. 202 and 209.

[13]Ibid., p. 204.

[14]Sara Davidson, *Loose Change* (New York: Pocket Books, 1978), p. 139.

[15]For a valuable discussion of this phenomenon, see June Singer, *Androgyny* (New York: Anchor Press/Doubleday,1976).

[16]*Life Against Death*, p. 30.

[17]The figure of the holy innocent can be clearly seen in the book which is the inspiration of *The Graduate* and indeed which forecasts this whole side of the sixties: J.D. Salinger's *The Catcher in the Rye*. Holden Caulfield considers himself a moron and is regarded as a failure; but his worldly failure is really the correlative of his spiritual superiority.

[18]"The Counterculture Trickster," *Psychocultural Review*, 2 (Winter, 1978), 53-61.

Index

www.ingramcontent.com/pod-product-compliance
Lightning Source LLC
Chambersburg PA
CBHW020417290526
45785CB00002B/607